Practice*Planners*

Arthur E. Jongsma, Jr., Series Editor

Helping therapists help their clients...

Practice*Planners*

Second Edition

THE COMPLETE ADULT
PSYCHOTHERAPY
Treatment Planner

A new, fully revised edition of the bestselling *The Complete Psychotherapy Treatment Planner*, this invaluable resource features:

• Treatment plan components for 39 behaviorally based problems—including five completely new problem sets

• A step-by-step guide to writing treatment plans

• Over 300 additional prewritten treatment goals, objectives, and interventions

• Handy workbook format with space to record your own treatment plan options

• Over 100,000 **Practice*Planners*** sold

Arthur E. Jongsma, Jr., and L. Mark Peterson

Practice*Planners*
Arthur E. Jongsma, Jr., Series Editor

Brief Therapy
HOMEWORK
PLANNER

• Contains 62 ready-to-copy homework assignments that can be used to facilitate brief individual therapy

• Homework assignments and exercises are keyed to over 39 behaviorally-based presenting problems from *The Complete Psychotherapy Treatment Planner*

• Assignments may be quickly customized using the enclosed disk

• Over 100,000 **Practice*Planners*** sold

Gary M. Schultheis

Practice*Planners*

The Clinical
DOCUMENTATION
SOURCEBOOK
Second Edition

A Comprehensive Collection of
Mental Health Practice
Forms, Handouts, and Records

FEATURES

• Contains ready-to-use forms for managing the mental health treatment process

• Covers every stage of the treatment process

• Includes customizable forms on disk

• Over 100,000 **Practice*Planners*** sold

Donald E. Wiger

Practice*Planners*
Arthur E. Jongsma, Jr., Series Editor

The Adult Psychotherapy
PROGRESS NOTES PLANNER

This time-saving resource:

• Contains Progress notes components for all behaviorally based problems

• Covers the gamut of possible outcomes to every objective suggested in the best-selling *Complete Adult Psychotherapy Treatment Planner, Second Edition*

• Follows a DSM-IV format that matches each problem set and is easy to record progress and outcomes

• Provides a handy workbook format with space to record your own progress notes options

• Over 100,000 **Practice*Planners*** sold

Arthur E. Jongsma, Jr.

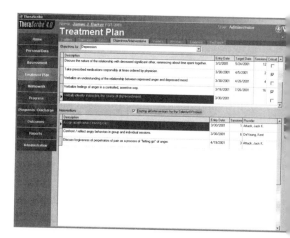

ractice*Planners*® Order Form

Treatment Planners cover all the necessary elements for developing formal treatment plans, including detailed problem definitions, long-term goals, short-term objectives, therapeutic interventions, and DSM-IV™ diagnoses.

❏ **The Complete Adult Psychotherapy Treatment Planner,** Second Edition
    0-471-31924-4 / $44.95

❏ **The Child Psychotherapy Treatment Planner,** Second Edition
    0-471-34764-7 / $44.95

❏ **The Adolescent Psychotherapy Treatment Planner,** Second Edition
    0-471-34766-3 / $44.95

❏ **The Addiction Treatment Planner,** Second Edition
    0-471-41814-5 / $44.95

❏ **The Couples Psychotherapy Treatment Planner**
    0-471-24711-1 / $44.95

❏ **The Group Therapy Treatment Planner**
    0-471-37449-0 / $44.95

❏ **The Family Therapy Treatment Planner**
    0-471-34768-X / $44.95

❏ **The Older Adult Psychotherapy Treatment Planner**
    0-471-29574-4 / $44.95

❏ **The Employee Assistance (EAP) Treatment Planner**
    0-471-24709-X / $44.95

❏ **The Gay and Lesbian Psychotherapy Treatment Planner**
    0-471-35080-X / $44.95

❏ **The Crisis Counseling and Traumatic Events Treatment Planner**
    0-471-39587-0 / $44.95

❏ **The Social Work and Human Services Treatment Planner**
    0-471-37741-4 / $44.95

❏ **The Continuum of Care Treatment Planner**
    0-471-19568-5 / $44.95

❏ **The Behavioral Medicine Treatment Planner**
    0-471-31923-6 / $44.95

❏ **The Mental Retardation and Developmental Disability Treatment Planner**
    0-471-38253-1 / $44.95

❏ **The Special Education Treatment Planner**
    0-471-38872-6 / $44.95

❏ **The Severe and Persistent Mental Illness Treatment Planner**
    0-471-35945-9 / $44.95

❏ **The Personality Disorders Treatment Planner**
    0-471-39403-3 / $44.95

❏ **The Rehabilitation Psychology Treatment Planner**
    0-471-35178-4 / $44.95

❏ **The Pastoral Counseling Treatment Planner**
    0-471-25416-9 / $44.95

❏ **The Juvenile Justice Treatment Planner**
    0-471-43320-9 / $44.95

❏ **The Psychiatric Evaluation & Psychopharmacology Treatment Planner**
    0-471-43322-5 / $44.95 (available 2/02)

❏ **The Adult Corrections Treatment Planner**
    0-471-20244-4 / $44.95 (available 6/02)

❏ **The School Counseling and School Social Work Treatment Planner**
    0-471-08496-4 / $44.95 (available 8/02)

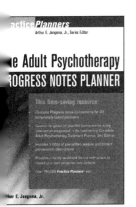

Progress Notes Planners contain complete prewritten progress notes for each presenting problem in the companion Treatment Planners.

❏ **The Adult Psychotherapy Progress Notes Planner**
    0-471-34763-9 / $44.95

❏ **The Adolescent Psychotherapy Progress Notes Planner**
    0-471-38104-7 / $44.95

❏ **The Child Psychotherapy Progress Notes Planner**
    0-471-38102-0 / $44.95

Name_____

Affiliation_____

Address_____

City/State/Zip_____

Phone/Fax_____

E-mail_____

To order, call 1-800-225-5945
(Please refer to promo #1-4019 when ordering.)

Or send this page with payment* to:
John Wiley & Sons, Inc., Attn: J. Knott
605 Third Avenue, New York, NY 10158-0012

❏ Check enclosed ❏ Visa ❏ MasterCard ❏ American Express

Card #_____

Expiration Date_____

Signature_____

On the web: practiceplanners.wiley.com

*Please add your local sales tax to all orders.

Practice **Planners**™

Arthur E. Jongsma, Jr., Series Editor

The Severe and Persistent Mental Illness Treatment Planner

David J. Berghuis

Arthur E. Jongsma, Jr.

JOHN WILEY & SONS, INC.

New York • Chichester • Weinheim • Brisbane • Singapore • Toronto

Copyright © 2000 by John Wiley & Sons. All rights reserved.
Published simultaneously in Canada.

Note about Photocopy Rights

The publisher grants purchasers permission to reproduce handouts from this book for professional use with their clients.

Library of Congress Cataloging-in-Publication Data:

Berghuis, David J.
 The severe and persistent mental illness treatment planner / David J. Berghuis, Arthur
E. Jongsma, Jr.
  p. cm. — (Practice planner series)
 ISBN 0-471-35945-9 (paper : alk. paper) — ISBN 0-471-35962-9 (paper/disk : alk. paper)
  1. Mentally ill—Rehabilitation—Planning—Handbooks, manuals, etc. 2. Chronically
ill—Rehabilitation—Planning—Handbooks, manuals, etc. 3. Psychiatric records—Forms.
I. Jongsma, Arthur E., 1943– II. Title. III. Practice planners.
 [DNLM: 1. Mental Disorders—therapy—Handbooks. 2. Chronic
Disease—therapy—Handbooks. 3. Patient Care Planning—Handbooks.
4. Psychotherapy—methods—Handbook. WM 34 B497s 2000]
RC480.53 .B47 2000
616.89'06—dc21

                        00-025006

Printed in the United States of America.

10 9 8 7 6 5 4

To my wife, Barbara, who patiently helps me to meet my potential and coordinates support for all areas of my life, and to my children, Katherine and Michael.

—David J. Berghuis

To all those kind and persistently attentive clinicians who provide treatment to the severely mentally ill who so often have been socially shunned and forgotten.

—Arthur E. Jongsma, Jr.

CONTENTS

SERIES PREFACE

The practice of psychotherapy has a dimension that did not exist 30, 20, or even 15 years ago—accountability. Treatment programs, public agencies, clinics, and even group and solo practitioners must now justify the treatment of patients to outside review entities that control the payment of fees. This development has resulted in an explosion of paperwork.

Clinicians must now document what has been done in treatment, what is planned for the future, and what the anticipated outcomes of the interventions are. The books and software in this Practice Planner series are designed to help practitioners fulfill these documentation requirements efficiently and professionally.

The Practice Planners series is growing rapidly. It now includes not only the original *Complete Psychotherapy Treatment Planner* and the *Child and Adolescent Psychotherapy Treatment Planner,* but also Treatment Planners targeted to specialty areas of practice, including: chemical dependency, the continuum of care, couples therapy, employee assistance, behavioral medicine, therapy with older adults, pastoral counseling, family therapy, group therapy, neuropsychology, therapy with gays and lesbians, and more.

In addition to the Treatment Planners, the series also includes Thera-Scribe®, the latest version of the popular treatment-planning and patient record-keeping software, as well as adjunctive books, such as the *Brief, Chemical Dependence, Couple, Child,* and *Adolescent Therapy Homework Planners, The Psychotherapy Documentation Primer,* and *Clinical, Forensic, Child, Couples and Family, Continuum of Care,* and *Chemical Dependence Documentation Sourcebooks*—containing forms and resources to aid in mental health practice management. The goal of the series is to provide practitioners with the resources they need to provide high-quality care in the era of accountability—or, to put it simply, we seek to help you spend more time on patients, and less time on paperwork.

ARTHUR E. JONGSMA, JR.
Grand Rapids, Michigan

PREFACE

The field of treatment for the severely and persistently mentally ill is at a pivotal point in its evolution. New medications have provided stability to people who have been chronically unstable in the past. What started with deinstitutionalization and the growth of community mental health centers has gradually transformed into a myriad of agencies and clinicians who provide treatment in a variety of settings. Many changes have also occurred for the agencies serving this population. In many areas, the service providers have been compelled to become more efficient and competitive for their clientele. Most agencies are required to obtain accrediation from outside auditors, such as the Joint Commission on the Accreditation of Health Organizations (JCAHO) or the Council on Accreditation (CARF). Payors often demand documentation of positive outcomes for clients whom we serve. With these many changes in the field, the need for better organization, treatment techniques, and documentation becomes self-evident.

To fill this need, we have developed *The Severe and Persistent Mental Illness Treatment Planner.* This new Planner suggests thousands of prewritten behavioral definitions, objectives, goals, and interventions for a variety of problem areas experienced by the men and women who suffer from chronic mental illness. This book will be useful to any clinician working with this population, but care has been taken to write from the perspective of the clinician who manages the client's entire treatment, whether he or she be called a case manager, supports coordinator, social worker, or some other name. Goals and interventions are written for a variety of types and levels of intensity of severe and persistent mental illnesses. It is our hope that this Planner will allow clinicians to quickly and accurately develop and implement helpful treatment plans for their clients.

It is also our hope that the compilation of therapeutic interventions will be helpful to clinicians who are struggling to find more efficient and innovative ways to help their clients reach their goals. This format is especially helpful by grouping a variety of different interventions together as they relate to one problem area. We hope that this will stimulate clinicians to develop new ways to solve old (and new) problems. However, because each client is different, this book should not be used in place of education, training, and clinical judgment and supervision.

A variety of people should be acknowledged for their assistance in developing this Planner. First, the clients who have been willing to share their lives and troubles have taught us more than can be written. Several staff members of the Community Mental Health Centers in Ionia County and Newaygo County (both in Michigan) have either knowingly or unknowingly provided feedback and ideas throughout the unfolding of this project. While developing this Planner, the authors were also involved in the writing of *The Mental Retardation and Developmental Disability Treatment Planner,* with Kellye Slaggert, M.A. Many ideas developed for that Planner were adapted for this one. Barbara Berghuis, wife of the primary author, and a case manager herself, was instrumental in developing and critiquing the manuscript throughout the process. The staff of the library of Calvin College and Seminary were invaluable in their assistance while researching material for this project. Jennifer Byrne has been a godsend throughout this project, brokering information between authors, adding and subtracting, sending, resending, and sending yet again through e-mail as each chapter has been developed.

No project this large gets completed without other priorities being rearranged. The willingness of our families to allow us to take the time to bring this idea to fruition is very much appreciated. It is their support and guidance that have allowed us to help others. Our editor at John Wiley & Sons, Kelly Franklin, has consistently provided us with supremely competent encouragement and guidance.

ARTHUR E. JONGSMA, JR.
DAVID J. BERGHUIS

INTRODUCTION

Since the early 1960s, formalized treatment planning has gradually become a vital aspect of the entire health care delivery system, whether it is treatment that is related to physical health, mental health, child welfare, or substance abuse. What started in the medical sector in the 1960s spread into the mental health sector in the 1970s as clinics, psychiatric hospitals, agencies, and so on, began to seek accreditation from bodies such as the Joint Commission on Accreditation of Healthcare Organizations (JCAHO) to qualify for third-party reimbursements. For most treatment providers to achieve accreditation, they had to begin developing and strengthening their documentation skills in the area of treatment planning. Previously, most mental health and substance abuse treatment providers had, at best, a "bare-bones" plan that looked similar for most of the individuals whom they treated. As a result, clients were uncertain about what they were trying to attain in mental health treatment. Goals were vague, objectives were nonexistent, and interventions were applied equally to all clients. Outcome data were not measurable, and neither the treatment provider nor the client knew exactly when treatment was complete. The initial development of rudimentary treatment plans made inroads toward addressing some of these issues.

With the advent of managed care in the 1980s, treatment planning has taken on even more importance. Managed care systems *insist* that clinicians move rapidly from assessment of the problem to the formulation and implementation of the treatment plan. The goal of most managed care companies is to expedite the treatment process by prompting the client and treatment provider to focus on identifying and changing behavioral problems as quickly as possible. Treatment plans must be specific as to the problems and interventions, individualized to meet the client's needs and goals, and measurable in terms of setting milestones that can be used to chart the client's progress. Pressure from third-party payers, accrediting agencies, and other outside parties has therefore increased the need for clinicians to produce effective, high-quality treatment plans in a short time frame. However, many mental health providers have little experience in treatment plan development. Our purpose in writing this book is to clarify, simplify, and accelerate the treatment planning process.

TREATMENT PLAN UTILITY

Detailed written treatment plans can benefit not only the client, therapist, treatment team, insurance community, and treatment agency, but also the overall mental health profession. The client is served by a written plan because it stipulates the issues that are the focus of the treatment process. It is very easy for both the provider and the client to lose sight of what the issues were that brought the client into treatment. The treatment plan is a guide that structures the focus of the therapeutic contract. Because issues can change as therapy progresses, the treatment plan must be viewed as a dynamic document that can and must be updated to reflect any major change of problem, definition, goal, objective, or intervention.

Clients and clinicians benefit from the treatment plan, which forces both to think about treatment outcomes. Behaviorally stated, measurable objectives clearly focus the treatment endeavor. Clients no longer have to wonder what treatment is trying to accomplish. Clear objectives also allow the client to channel effort into specific changes that will lead to the long-term goal of problem resolution. Treatment is no longer a vague contract to try to solve problem areas. Both the client and the therapist are concentrating on specifically stated objectives using specific interventions.

Providers are aided by treatment plans because they are forced to think analytically and critically about therapeutic interventions that are best suited for objective attainment for the client. Clinicians were traditionally trained to coordinate the client's needs, but now a formalized plan is the guide to the treatment process. The clinician must give advance attention to the technique, approach, assignment, or referral that will form the basis for interventions.

Clinicians benefit from clear documentation of treatment because it provides a measure of added protection from possible client litigation. Malpractice suits are increasing in frequency and insurance premiums are soaring. The first line of defense against allegations is a complete clinical record detailing the treatment process. A written, individualized, formal treatment plan that is the guideline for the therapeutic process, that has been reviewed and signed by the client, and that is coupled with problem-oriented progress notes is a powerful defense against exaggerated or false claims.

A well-crafted treatment plan that clearly stipulates presenting problems and intervention strategies facilitates the treatment process that is carried out by team members in inpatient, residential, or intensive outpatient settings. Good communication between team members about what approach is being implemented and who is responsible for which intervention is critical. Team meetings to discuss client treatment used to be the only source of interaction between providers; often, therapeutic conclusions or assignments were not recorded. Now, a thorough treatment plan stipulates in writing the details of objectives and the varied interventions (pharmacologic, group therapy, didactic, recreational, individual therapy, and so on) and who will implement them.

Every treatment agency or institution is constantly looking for ways to increase the quality and uniformity of the documentation in the clinical record. A standardized, written treatment plan with problem definitions, goals, objectives, and interventions in every client's file enhances that uniformity of documentation. This uniformity eases the task of record reviewers inside and outside the agency. Outside reviewers, such as JCAHO, insist on documentation that clearly outlines assessment, treatment, progress, and discharge status.

The demand for accountability from third-party payers and oversight organizations is partially satisfied by a written treatment plan and complete progress notes. More and more outside reviewers are demanding a structured therapeutic contract that has measurable objectives and explicit interventions. Clinicians cannot avoid this move toward being accountable to those outside the treatment process.

The mental health profession stands to benefit from the use of more precise, measurable objectives to evaluate success in mental health treatment. With the advent of detailed treatment plans, outcome data can be collected more easily for interventions that are effective in achieving specific goals.

HOW TO DEVELOP A TREATMENT PLAN

The process of developing a treatment plan involves a logical series of steps that build on each other, much like constructing a house. The foundation of any effective treatment plan is the data that are gathered in a thorough biopsychosocial assessment. As the client presents himself or herself for treatment, the clinician must sensitively listen to and understand what the client struggles with in terms of family-of-origin issues, current stressors, emotional status, social network, physical health, coping skills, interpersonal conflicts, self-esteem, and so on. Assessment data may be gathered from a social history, physical exam, clinical interview, psychological testing, or contact with a client's significant others. The integration of the data by the clinician or the multidisciplinary treatment team members is critical for understanding the client, as is an awareness of the basis of the client's struggle. We have identified six specific steps for developing an effective treatment plan that is based on the assessment data.

Step One: Problem Selection

Although the client may discuss a variety of issues during the assessment, the clinician must ferret out the most significant problems on which to focus the treatment process. Usually, a *primary* problem will surface, and *secondary* problems may also be evident. Some *other* problems may have to be set aside as not urgent enough to require treatment at this time. An effective treatment plan can only deal with a few selected problems, or treatment will lose its direction. This Planner offers 25 problems from which to select those that most accurately represent your client's presenting issues.

As the problems to be selected become clear to the clinician or the treatment team, it is important to include opinions from the client as to his or her prioritization of issues for which help is being sought. A client's motivation to participate in and cooperate with the treatment process depends, to some extent, on the degree to which treatment addresses his or her greatest needs.

Step Two: Problem Definition

Each individual client presents with unique nuances as to how a problem reveals itself behaviorally in his or her life. Therefore, each problem that is selected for treatment focus requires a specific definition about how it is evidenced in the particular client. The symptom pattern may be associated with diagnostic criteria and codes such as those found in the *Diagnostic and Statistical Manual* or the *International Classification of Diseases*. The Planner, following the pattern established by *DSM-IV,* offers such behaviorally specific definition statements to choose from or to serve as a model for your own personally crafted statements. You will find several behavior symptoms or syndromes listed that may characterize one of the 25 presenting problems.

Step Three: Goal Development

The next step in treatment plan development is that of setting broad goals for the resolution of the target problem. These statements need not be crafted in measurable terms but can be global, long-term goals that indicate a desired positive outcome to the treatment procedures. The Planner suggests several possible goal statements for each problem, but one statement is all that is required in a treatment plan.

Step Four: Objective Construction

In contrast to long-term goals, objectives must be stated in behaviorally measurable language. It must be clear when the client has achieved the established objectives; therefore, vague, subjective objectives are not acceptable. Review agencies (e.g., JCAHO) and managed care organizations insist that psychological treatment outcome be measurable. The objectives that are presented in this Planner are designed to meet this demand for accountability. Numerous alternatives are presented to allow construction of a variety of treatment plan possibilities for the same presenting problem. The clinician must exercise professional judgment as to which objectives are most appropriate for a given client.

Each objective should be developed as a step toward attaining the broad treatment goal. In essence, objectives can be thought of as a series of steps that, when completed, will result in the achievement of the long-term goal. There should be at least two objectives for each problem, but the clinician may construct as many as are necessary for goal achievement. Target attainment dates may be listed for each objective. New objectives should be added to the plan as the individual's treatment progresses. When all of the necessary objectives have been achieved, the client should have resolved the target problem successfully.

Step Five: Intervention Creation

Interventions are the clinician's actions that are designed to help the client complete the objectives. There should be at least one intervention for every objective. If the client does not accomplish the objective after the initial intervention, new interventions should be added to the plan. Interventions should be selected on the basis of the client's needs and the treatment provider's full therapeutic repertoire. This Planner contains interventions from a broad range of therapeutic approaches, including psychotherapeutic, didactic training, bibliotherapy, family interventions, and linking to outside resources. Other interventions may be written by the provider to reflect his or her own training and experience. The addition of new problems, definitions, goals, objectives, and interventions to those that are found in the Planner is encouraged because doing so adds to the database for future reference and use.

Some suggested interventions listed in the Planner refer to specific books that can be assigned to the client for adjunctive bibliotherapy. Appendix A contains a full bibliographic reference list of these materials. The books are arranged under each problem for which they are appropriate as assigned reading for clients. When a book is used as part of an intervention plan, it should be reviewed with the client after it is read, enhancing the application of the book's content to the specific client's circumstances. For further information about self-help books, mental health professionals may wish to consult *The Authoritative Guide to Self-Help Books* (1994) by Santrock, Minnett, and Campbell (available from The Guilford Press, New York).

Assigning an intervention to a specific provider is most relevant if the client is being treated by a team in an inpatient, residential, intensive outpatient, or other treatment team setting. Within these settings, personnel other than the primary clinician may be responsible for implementing a specific intervention. Review agencies require that the responsible provider's name be stipulated for every intervention.

Step Six: Diagnosis Determination

The determination of an appropriate diagnosis is based on an evaluation of the client's complete clinical presentation. The clinician must compare the behavioral, cognitive, emotional, and interpersonal symptoms that the client presents with the criteria for diagnosis of a mental illness condition as described in *DSM-IV*. The issue of differential diagnosis is admittedly a difficult one that research has shown to have rather low interrater reliability. Psychologists have also been trained to think more in terms of maladaptive behavior than in disease labels. In spite of these factors, diagnosis is a reality that exists in the world of mental health care, and it is a necessity for third-party reimbursement. (However, recently, managed care agencies are more interested in behavioral indices that are exhibited by the client than in the actual diagnosis.) It is the clinician's thorough knowledge of *DSM-IV* criteria and a complete understanding of the client assessment data that contribute to the most reliable, valid diagnosis. An accurate assessment of behavioral indicators will also contribute to more effective treatment planning.

HOW TO USE THIS PLANNER

Our experience has taught us that learning the skills of effective treatment plan writing can be a tedious and difficult process for many clinicians. It is more stressful to try to develop this expertise when under the pressure of increased client load and other productivity pressures. The documentation demands can be overwhelming when we must move quickly from assessment to treatment plan to progress notes. In the process, we must be very specific about how and when objectives can be achieved, and how progress is exhibited in each client. *The Severe and Persistent Mental Illness Treatment Planner* was developed as a tool to aid clinicians in writing a treatment plan in a rapid manner that is clear, specific, and highly individualized according to the following progression:

1. Choose one presenting problem (Step One) that you have identified through your assessment process. Locate the corresponding page number for that problem in the Planner's table of contents.

2. Select two or three of the listed behavioral definitions (Step Two) and record them in the appropriate section on your treatment plan form. Feel free to add your own defining statement if you determine that your client's behavioral manifestation of the identified problem is not listed. (Note that although our design for treatment planning is vertical, it will work equally well on plan forms that are formatted horizontally.)

3. Select a single long-term goal (Step Three) and again write the selection, exactly as it is written in the Planner or in some appropriately modified form, in the corresponding area of your own form.

4. Review the listed objectives for this problem and select the ones that you judge to be clinically indicated for your client (Step Four). Remember, it is recommended that you select at least two objectives for each problem. Add a target date or the number of sessions that have been allocated for the attainment of each objective.

5. Choose relevant interventions (Step Five). The Planner offers suggested interventions that are related to each objective in the parentheses following the objective statement. However, do not limit yourself to those interventions. The entire list is eclectic and may offer options that are more tailored to your theoretical approach or preferred way of working with clients. Also, just as with definitions, goals, and objectives, there is space allowed for you to enter your own interventions into the Planner. This allows you to refer to these entries when you create a plan around this problem in the future. You will have to assign responsibility to a specific person for the implementation of each intervention if the treatment is being carried out by a multidisciplinary team.

6. Several *DSM-IV* diagnoses are listed at the end of each chapter that are commonly associated with a client who has this prob-

lem. These diagnoses are meant to be suggestions for clinical consideration. Select a diagnosis that is listed or assign a more appropriate choice from the *DSM-IV* (Step Six).

Note: To accommodate those practitioners who tend to plan treatment in terms of diagnostic labels rather than presenting problems, Appendix B lists all of the *DSM-IV* diagnoses that have been presented in the various presenting problem chapters as suggestions for consideration. Each diagnosis is followed by the presenting problem that has been associated with that diagnosis. The provider may look up the presenting problems for a selected diagnosis to review definitions, goals, objectives, and interventions that may be appropriate for their clients with that diagnosis. Congratulations! You should now have a complete, individualized treatment plan that is ready for immediate implementation and presentation to the client. It should resemble the format of the sample plan presented on page 10.

A FINAL NOTE

One important aspect of effective treatment planning is that each plan should be tailored to the individual client's problems and needs. Treatment plans should not be mass-produced, even if clients have similar problems. The individual's strengths and weaknesses, unique stressors, social network, family circumstances, and symptom patterns *must* be considered in developing a treatment strategy. Drawing upon our own years of clinical experience, we have put together a variety of treatment choices. These statements can be combined in thousands of permutations to develop detailed treatment plans. Relying on their own good judgment, clinicians can easily select the statements that are appropriate for the individuals whom they are treating. In addition, we encourage readers to add their own definitions, goals, objectives, and interventions to the existing samples. It is our hope that *The Severe and Persistent Mental Illness Treatment Planner* will promote effective, creative treatment planning—a process that will ultimately benefit the client, clinician, and mental health community.

SUMMARY

Effective treatment plan writing is becoming increasingly important. We have put together a variety of choices to allow for thousands of potential combinations of statements that join to make a completed plan for treatment. Clinicians with their good judgment can easily select statements that are appropriate for the individuals whom they are treating. Each statement can be modified as necessary to apply more directly to a specific individual client. Finally, we believe from our experience that the Planner method of treatment plan construction is helpful in that it stimulates creative thoughts by clinicians. New ideas for all components of a treatment plan may come to mind as the Planner statements are reviewed. Clinicians can add to the Planner by writing in new definitions, goals, objectives, and interventions.

SAMPLE TREATMENT PLAN

PROBLEM: MEDICATION MANAGEMENT

Definitions: Failure to consistently take psychotropic medications as prescribed.

Verbalization of fears and dislike related to physical and/or emotional side effects of prescribed medications.

Failure to respond as expected to a prescribed medication regimen.

Goals: Regular, consistent use of psychotropic medications at the prescribed dosage, frequency, and duration.

Increased understanding of the psychotropic medication dosage, the side effects, and the reasons for being prescribed.

Objectives	Interventions
1. Take psychotropic medications as prescribed.	1. Arrange for a psychiatric evaluation to assess the need for new or additional psychiatric medications.
	2. Provide a written description to the client of his/her medications, the acceptable dosage levels, and the side effects.
2. Verbalize accurate information regarding the reasons for, the side effects of, and the expected outcome of prescribed medications.	1. Request that the client identify the reason for the use of each medication; correct any misinformation.
	2. Refer the client to a physician, a pharmacist, or other medical staff for additional information on specific medications.
3. Report to the appropriate professional the side effects and the effectiveness of the medications.	1. Monitor the client's use of and expected benefits of the medications.
	2. Review the side effects of the medication with the client and the medical staff.
	3. Obtain a written release of information from the client to his/her primary physician or other health care providers to

(Continued)

inform them of the medications and the expected side effects, risks, and benefits.

4. Arrange for the client to receive information about lifestyle habits (i.e., tobacco use,
diet) that can be modified to
decrease the side effects of the
medication.

4. Identify the beliefs that are
barriers to proper medication
usage.

1. Request that the client describe fears that he/she may
experience regarding the use
of the medication. Process
these fears, correcting myths
and misinformation.

2. Request that the client identify social concerns that he/she
may experience regarding
medication usage (i.e., stigmatization, loss of independence).

5. Attend a support group for the
mentally ill.

1. Refer the client to a support
group for individuals with severe and persistent mental illness.

6. Verbalize positive feelings
about the improvement that is
resulting from the medication's effectiveness.

1. Request that the client identify
how the reduction in mental
illness symptoms has improved
his/her social or family system.

Diagnosis: 295.10   Schizophrenia, Disorganized Type

Note: The numbers in parentheses accompanying the short-term objectives in each chapter correspond to the list of suggested therapeutic interventions in that chapter. Each objective has specific interventions that
have been designed to assist the client in attaining that objective. Clinical judgment should determine the exact intervention to be used, including any outside of those suggested.

ACTIVITIES OF DAILY LIVING (ADL)

BEHAVIORAL DEFINITIONS

1. Substandard hygiene and grooming, as evidenced by strong body odor, disheveled hair, or dirty clothing.
2. Failure to use basic hygiene techniques, such as bathing, brushing teeth, or washing clothes.
3. Medical problems due to poor hygiene.
4. Poor diet due to deficiencies in cooking, meal preparation, or food selection.
5. Impaired reality testing resulting in bizarre behaviors that compromise ability to perform activities of daily living (ADLs).
6. Poor interaction skills as evidenced by limited eye contact, insufficient attending, and awkward social responses.
7. History of others excusing the client's poor performance on ADLs due to factors that are not related to his/her mental illness.
8. Inadequate knowledge or functioning in basic skills around the home (e.g., cleaning floors, washing dishes, disposing of garbage, keeping fresh food available, etc.).
9. Loss of relationships, employment, or other social opportunities due to poor hygiene and inadequate attention to grooming.

—. _____
   _____
   _____
—. _____
   _____
   _____
—. _____
   _____

LONG-TERM GOALS

1. Increase functioning in ADLs in a consistent and responsible manner.
2. Understand the need for good hygiene and implement healthy personal hygiene practices.
3. Learn basic skills for maintaining a clean, sanitary living space.
4. Regularly shower or bathe, shave, brush teeth, care for hair, and use deodorant.
5. Experience increased social acceptance because of improved appearance or functioning in ADLs.
6. Family, friends, and caregivers provide healthy feedback to the client regarding ADLs.

—. _____
   _____
   _____
—. _____
   _____
   _____
—. _____
   _____

SHORT-TERM OBJECTIVES

1. Describe current functioning in ADLs. (1, 2, 3)
2. List the negative effects of not giving enough effort to responsible performance of ADLs. (2, 4, 5, 6)
3. Express emotions related to impaired ADL performance. (4, 7)
4. Verbalize insight into the secondary gain that is associated with decreased ADL functioning. (8)
5. Prioritize those ADL areas upon which to focus effort and improve functioning. (1, 2, 9, 10)

THERAPEUTIC INTERVENTIONS

1. Request that the client prepare an inventory of positive and negative functioning regarding ADLs.
2. Ask the client to identify a trusted individual from whom he/she can obtain helpful feedback regarding daily hygiene and cleanliness. Coordinate feedback from this individual to the client.
3. Refer the client to a dietician for an assessment regarding basic nutritional knowledge and skills, usual diet, and nutritional deficiencies.

6. Identify any cognitive barriers to ADL success. (11)

7. Participate in a remediation program to teach ADL skills. (12)

8. Acknowledge ADL deficits as a symptom of mental illness being inadequately controlled or treated. (13, 14)

9. Stabilize, through the use of psychotropic medications, psychotic and other severe and persistent mental illness symptoms that interfere with ADLs. (15, 16, 17)

10. Use medication reminders to improve compliance with the prescribed regimen. (16, 17, 18)

11. Agree to the need for and cooperate with medication administration by a family or staff member. (19)

12. Report the side effects and effectiveness of prescribed medications to the appropriate professional. (16, 17, 20)

13. Remediate the medical effects that have resulted from a history of a lack of ADL performance. (21, 22)

14. Implement skills that are related to basic personal hygiene on a consistent daily basis. (23, 24, 25, 26)

15. Utilize a self-monitoring system to increase the frequency of regular use of basic hygiene skills. (27, 28, 29)

16. Utilize community resources to improve personal hygiene and grooming. (30, 31)

4. Ask the client to identify two painful experiences in which rejection was experienced (e.g., broken relationships, loss of employment) due to the lack of performance of basic ADLs.

5. Help the client to visualize or imagine the possible positive changes that could occur from increased attention to appearance and other daily living skills.

6. Review with the client the medical risks (e.g., dental problems, risk of infection, lice, etc.) that are associated with poor hygiene or lack of attention to other ADLs.

7. Assist the client to express emotions related to impaired performance in ADLs (e.g., embarrassment, depression, low self-esteem, etc.).

8. Reflect the possible secondary gain (e.g., less involvement in potentially difficult social situations) that is associated with decreased ADL functioning.

9. Ask the client to identify or describe those ADLs that are desired but are not present in the current repertoire.

10. Facilitate the client prioritizing the implementation of ADLs or the learning of skills that are necessary to implement these ADLs.

11. Refer the client for an assessment of cognitive abilities and deficits.

17. Terminate substance abuse that interferes with the ability to care for self. (32, 33, 34)
18. Implement basic skills for running and maintaining a home or apartment. (35, 36)
19. Report as to the schedule that is adhered to regarding the regular use of housekeeping skills. (27, 28, 37, 38)
20. Implement basic cooking skills and eat nutritionally balanced meals daily. (3, 39, 40, 41, 42)
21. Engage in physical exercise several times per week. (21, 43, 44, 45, 46)
22. Take steps to increase safety and health in the home setting. (47, 48, 49, 50)
23. Terminate engagement in high-risk sex or substance abuse behaviors. (32, 51, 52)
24. Acknowledge that severe mental illness symptoms can present a safety problem for self or others. (53)
25. Sign an intervention action plan that will be implemented when cognitive decompensation begins. (54)
26. Caregivers implement stress reduction behaviors. (55, 56, 57)

__. _____
_____
__. _____
_____
__. _____
_____

12. Recommend remediating programs to the client, such as skill-building groups, token economies, or behavior-shaping programs that are focused on removing deficits to ADL performance.
13. Educate the client about the expected or common symptoms of his/her mental illness (e.g., manic excitement or negative symptoms of schizophrenia), which may negatively impact basic ADL functioning.
14. Reflect or interpret poor performance in ADLs as an indicator of psychiatric decompensation; share observations with the client, with caregivers, and with medical staff.
15. Arrange for an evaluation of the client by a physician for a prescription for psychotropic medication.
16. Educate the client about the proper use and the expected benefits of psychotropic medication.
17. Monitor the client for compliance with the psychotropic medication that is prescribed and for its effectiveness and possible side effects.
18. Provide the client with a pillbox for organizing and coordinating each dose of medications. Teach and quiz the client about the proper use of the medication com-

pliance package/reminder system.

19. Coordinate the family members or caregivers who will regularly dispense and/or monitor the client's medication compliance.

20. Review the possible side effects of the medication with the client and report any significant incidence to the medical staff.

21. Arrange for a full physical examination of the client, and encourage the physician to prescribe any necessary ADL remediation behaviors.

22. Refer the client to a dentist to determine dental treatment needs. Coordinate ongoing dental treatment.

23. Provide the client with written or video educational material for basic personal hygiene skills (e.g., *The Complete Guide to Better Dental Care* by Taintor and Taintor or *The New Wellness Encyclopedia* by the editors of the University of California-Berkeley).

24. Refer the client to an agency medical staff for one-to-one training in basic hygiene needs and techniques.

25. Conduct or refer the client to a psychoeducational group for teaching personal hygiene skills. Use the group setting to help teach the client to give and re-

ceive feedback about hygiene skill implementation.

26. Encourage and reinforce the client for performing basic hygiene skills on a regular schedule (e.g., at the same time and in the same order each day).

27. Refer the client to a behavioral treatment specialist to develop and implement a program to monitor and reward the regular use of ADL techniques.

28. Help the client to develop a self-monitoring program (e.g., a checkoff chart for ADL needs).

29. Provide the client with regular feedback about progress in his/her use of self-monitoring to improve personal hygiene.

30. Review the use of community resources with the client (e.g., laundromat/ dry cleaner, hair salon/ barber, etc.) that can be used to improve personal appearance.

31. Coordinate for the client to tour community facilities for cleaning and pressing clothes, cutting and styling hair, or purchasing soap and deodorant, with an emphasis on increasing the client's understanding of this service and how it can be used.

32. Assess the client for substance abuse that exacerbates poor ADL performance.

33. Refer the client to Alcoholics Anonymous (AA), Narcotics Anonymous (NA), or other substance abuse treatment options. (See the Chemical Dependence chapter in this Planner.)

34. Provide integrated, coordinated mental health and substance abuse treatment services.

35. Facilitate family members, friends, and caregivers who are training the client in basic housekeeping skills, and monitor his/her progress.

36. Teach the client basic housekeeping skills, utilizing references such as *Mary Ellen's Complete Home Reference Book* (Pinkham and Burg) or *The Cleaning Encyclopedia* (Aslett).

37. Provide the client with feedback about the care of his/her personal area, apartment, or home.

38. Encourage family members and caregivers to provide regular assignment of basic chores around the home.

39. Educate the client on basic cooking techniques (e.g., see portions of *The Good Housekeeping Illustrated Cookbook* by the editors of *Good Housekeeping* or *How to Cook Everything* by Bittman).

40. Refer the client to or conduct a psychoeducational

group regarding cooking skills and dietary needs.

41. Monitor the client's follow-through regarding a dietician's recommendations for changes in the client's cooking and eating practices.

42. Facilitate the client's enrollment in a community education cooking class or seminar.

43. Refer the client to an activity therapist for recommendations regarding physical fitness activities that are available in the community or through health clubs and so forth.

44. Assist the client in setting specific exercise goals and monitor his/her participation in exercise and physical fitness activities.

45. Provide educational material, such as *Fitness and Health* (Sharkey) or *ACSM Fitness Book* (American College of Sports Medicine), to increase knowledge of physical fitness needs.

46. Coordinate or facilitate a membership for the client at a local health club or YMCA/YWCA program.

47. Join the client in an inspection of his/her living situation for potential safety hazards.

48. Assist the client in advocating with the landlord, home provider, or family members to remediate safety haz-

ards, insect infestations, and so on.

49. Prioritize safety concerns around the client's home. Assist the client in developing and implementing plans to make the home a safer environment.

50. Facilitate the client's involvement with programs that assist low-income or special-needs individuals with safety equipment (e.g., free smoke or carbon monoxide detectors).

51. Teach the client about high-risk sexual behaviors and refer to a free condom program. (See the Sexuality Concerns chapter in this Planner.)

52. Teach the client about the serious risk that is involved with sharing needles for drug abuse; refer the client to needle exchange and substance abuse treatment programs.

53. Point out to the client his/her behaviors that appear to be signs of psychosis, mania, or other severe and persistent mental illness, and that could increase the potential for harm to self or others or decrease the ability to care for his/her own basic needs (ADLs).

54. Develop a written, signed intervention plan (e.g., call a treatment hotline, contact a therapist or a physician, go to a hospital emergency

department, etc.) to decrease the potential for injury, poisoning, or other self-care problems during periods of mania, psychosis, or other decompensation.

55. Assess the need for the client's transfer to an alternative care setting, or for the use of a respite provider.

56. Provide training to the caregiver on the client's pertinent diagnostic symptoms, as well as techniques for the caregiver's personal stress management.

57. Refer the caregiver to a stress management or support group for providers.

—. _____
   _____

—. _____
   _____

—. _____
   _____

DIAGNOSTIC SUGGESTIONS

Axis I:		
	297.1	Delusional Disorder
	295.xx	Schizophrenia
	295.10	Schizophrenia, Disorganized Type
	295.30	Schizophrenia, Paranoid Type
	295.90	Schizophrenia, Undifferentiated Type
	295.60	Schizophrenia, Residual Type
	295.70	Schizoaffective Disorder
	296.xx	Bipolar I Disorder
	296.89	Bipolar II Disorder
	_____	_____
	_____	_____

AGING

BEHAVIORAL DEFINITIONS

1. Advanced age that is debilitating to independent functioning.
2. Decreased intensity of severe and persistent mental illness symptoms.
3. Cognitive decline, including memory problems, confusion, or an inability to learn new information.
4. Loss of social support system due to infirmity or death of members of family of origin and friends.
5. Receives little or no interest in or support for self from offspring.
6. Medical problems related to advanced age.
7. Physical deficits due to long-term use of psychiatric medications (e.g., tardive dyskinesia).
8. Spiritual confusion leads to uncertainty about the meaning or purpose in life and fears surrounding mortality issues.
9. Decreased ability to perform ADLs or independent activities of daily living (IADLs).
10. Increased suicidal ideation.
11. Increased vulnerability to sexual, physical, and psychological abuse.
12. Anger outbursts due to frustration over declining abilities.

___. _____

_____

___. _____

_____

___. _____

_____

LONG-TERM GOALS

1. Stabilize medical status.
2. Decrease the slope or severity of cognitive decline.
3. Accept the loss of loved ones and other important individuals.
4. Develop additional social/emotional support systems.
5. Decrease the effects of long-term use of medications.
6. Terminate suicidal ideation and increase satisfaction with life.
7. Increased ability to resist abuse.
8. Express emotions in a healthy, safe manner.

—. _____
   _____
   _____
—. _____
   _____
   _____
—. _____
   _____

SHORT-TERM OBJECTIVES

1. Identify problematic changes that are related to the aging process. (1, 2, 3)
2. Express emotions regarding the aging process. (2, 4, 5, 6, 7)
3. Identify positive aspects of senior citizen status. (8, 9, 10)
4. Cooperate with a medical evaluation and follow through on obtaining treatment for physical health difficulties. (11, 12)
5. Express physical health concerns to medical staff. (3, 11, 13, 14)
6. Verbalize an understanding of physical health difficul-

THERAPEUTIC INTERVENTIONS

1. Request that the client identify negative situations that have occurred due to aging issues.
2. Request that the client list fears about impending issues related to the aging process.
3. Provide the client with general information regarding the aging process; recommend books such as *The Practical Guide to Aging* by Cassel or *Alzheimer's and Dementia: Questions You Have . . . Answers You Need* by Hay.
4. Request the client to identify his/her emotions regard-

ties and the recovery process. (15, 16)

7. Cooperate with a physician's evaluation as to the need for a change in or initiation of psychotropic medication. (17, 18, 19)

8. Report the side effects and effectiveness of prescribed medications to the appropriate professional. (18, 19, 20)

9. Take all medications safely and as medically prescribed. (12, 17, 21, 22, 23)

10. Authorize and encourage all physicians who are prescribing medications for self to communicate with each other and coordinate their medications. (22, 23, 24, 25)

11. Preserve independence by maintaining ADLs and IADLs. (26, 27)

12. Attend and participate in an auditory and/or vision evaluation. (28, 29)

13. Move to a supervised residential environment that meets psychiatric, physical, and cognitive needs. (27, 30, 31, 32, 33)

14. Express and report a resolution of grief associated with losses of loved ones, capabilities, freedom, or other attachment. (34, 35, 36, 37)

15. Make at least two social contacts on a daily basis to reduce isolation. (30, 38, 39, 40, 41)

16. As severe and persistent mental illness symptoms

ing aging issues (e.g., fear of abandonment, sadness regarding loss of abilities).

5. Teach the client healthy ways to express anger, such as writing, drawing, or empty-chair techniques. (See the Anger Management chapter in this Planner).

6. Coordinate training for the caregivers in physical management and anger diffusion techniques.

7. Teach the client stress management techniques (e.g., assertiveness and relaxation) that he/she can implement to prevent anxiety response.

8. Assist the client in preparing a list of benefits that are related to the aging process (e.g., decreased work expectations, new residential opportunities).

9. Give feedback to the client regarding the decreased expectations and stress level that older adults often experience.

10. Provide the client with specific information about the aging process and his/her mental illness (e.g., the tendency for severe and persistent mental illness symptoms to decrease in intensity in later years).

11. Refer the client for a complete physical evaluation by a medical staff who is knowledgeable in both geri-

abate, increase involvement in activities that were previously contraindicated due to psychotic symptomatology. (10, 42, 43, 44)

17. State a plan that is focused on repairing and restoring lost relationships as functioning improves. (38, 45, 46)

18. Report reduced anxiety regarding changes in occupational status due to retirement or aging. (4, 9, 44, 47, 48)

19. Caregivers share their frustrations associated with supervising a person with psychosis. (49, 50, 51, 52)

20. Describe incidents of being physically, emotionally, sexually, or financially abused. (53, 54, 55)

21. Terminate contact with perpetrators of physical, sexual, or emotional abuse. (56, 57, 58, 59)

22. Report a meaningful connection to a spiritual power beyond self. (60, 61, 62)

23. Develop a plan for care prior to age-related decompensation. (63, 64, 65)

__. _____
_____
__. _____
_____
__. _____
_____

atric and mental illness concerns.

12. Support and monitor the client in following up on the recommendations from the medical evaluation, such as pursuing specialty evaluations, lab work, medications, or other treatments.

13. Assist the client in expressing physical health needs to the medical staff (e.g., "translate" the client's bizarre descriptions to the medical staff, role-play asking questions of or reporting concerns to the medical staff, etc.).

14. Interpret psychiatric decompensation as a possible reaction to medical instability and the stress that is associated with it. Inquire about medical needs when the client has decompensated psychiatrically.

15. After obtaining the necessary confidentiality release from the client or his/her guardian, obtain information about physical health concerns from the attending physician.

16. Review health concerns and recovery needs with the client on a regular basis. Quiz the client about his/her understanding of these issues.

17. Arrange for an evaluation by a physician as to the necessity for a change in or the initiation of a prescrip-

tion for psychotropic medication.

18. Educate the client about the use and expected benefits of the medication.

19. Monitor the client's medication compliance.

20. Review the side effects of the medication with the client and the medical staff.

21. Assess the client's ability to adhere consistently to the prescribed regimen for all medications.

22. Provide the client with assistance in coordinating medications (e.g., a dose-by-dose pillbox or some other compliance packaging and reminder system that the pharmacist can recommend).

23. Count the amount of medications that the client currently has available, which should correspond with the amount that remains if the prescription regimen has been followed; review discrepancies with the client and the medical staff.

24. Coordinate authorizations to release confidential information so that multiple physicians can communicate with each other regarding the medications that are prescribed.

25. Facilitate the exchange of information between multiple physicians regarding medications prescribed for

the client and their possible chemical interaction.

26. Coordinate an evaluation of ADLs and IADLs, identifying strengths, weaknesses, and expected future levels of functioning.

27. Develop supports for maintenance of ADLs/IADLs from family, community, and paid staff. [See Activities of Daily Living (ADL) chapter in this Planner.]

28. Inquire about hearing or vision needs when the client complains about the increase in auditory and visual hallucinations, particularly when they are not accompanied by other severe and persistent mental illness symptoms.

29. Refer the client for auditory and vision exams.

30. Refer the client to an appropriate supervised residential option (e.g., independent living senior citizens' center, assisted living center, adult foster care, or nursing home).

31. Advocate with age-appropriate housing programs to accept the client and to provide needed adaptations for him/her.

32. Provide training to the housing staff about how to assist the mentally ill resident.

33. Acknowledge with the client his/her history of institutionalization. Help him/her

to differentiate between previous psychiatric hospitalizations and a move from hard-won independence into a more restrictive residential placement due to aging concerns.

34. Explore with the client his/her history of significant loss due to death, geographical move, aging, or physical/ mental disability; provide the client with support and empathy regarding the losses.

35. Educate the client about the grief process, and how these concerns may impact his/her severe and persistent mental illness symptoms.

36. Refer the client for individual therapy regarding the history of his/her losses.

37. Coordinate involvement in a support group for grief and loss issues, chronic mental illness concerns, or both.

38. Assist the client in developing social skills. (See Social Skills chapter in this Planner.)

39. Coordinate or link the client to age-appropriate social activities.

40. Refer the client to a recreational therapist for an evaluation of recreational abilities, needs, and opportunities.

41. Attune the client to the need to self-regulate his/her social involvement depending on his/her needs and

symptoms (e.g., increase or decrease frequency and intensity of contacts to modulate stress level).

42. Review the client's history of symptoms, using medical records as needed. Assist the client in making a timeline of mental illness concerns (e.g., onset, diagnostic changes, hospitalizations, or key recovery points).

43. Assist the client in identifying how severe and persistent mental illness symptoms have decreased as he/she is growing older.

44. Assist the client in identifying activities in which he/she can now be engaged as psychotic symptoms gradually abate.

45. Request that the client identify the important relationships that he/she would like to restore.

46. Assist the client in developing a plan for restoring relationships. (See either the Social Skills or the Family Conflicts chapters in this Planner.)

47. Normalize the changes that are occurring in the client's occupational situation through usual milestones (e.g., a retirement party, transition to volunteering, or leisure activities).

48. Provide the client with information and feedback about his/her changing roles and

planning for later years (e.g., *Simplifying Life as a Senior Citizen* by Cleveland).

49. Provide the family and the caregiver with adequate information and training relative to the client's mental illness, physical health, and aging concerns (recommend *Surviving Schizophrenia* by Torrey or *Helping Someone With Mental Illness* by Carter and Golant).

50. Allow the caregiver to vent about difficulties that are related to caring for the client. Listen with empathy, eventually focusing the caregiver toward developing alternative plans for the client's care or committing to continue the care. Do not allow the caregiver to deride the client.

51. Educate the caregivers and family members about programs, techniques, and options for caring for older adults. (Refer them to guidebooks such as *Coping With Your Difficult Older Parent* by Lebow, Kane, and Lebow, or *The Hospice Handbook* by Beresford.)

52. Refer the caregiver to a support group for those who care for the chronically mentally ill, the aged, or both.

53. Assess the client for the possibility of him/her being a victim of elder abuse in any form.

54. Explore with the client the details of any physical, emotional, sexual, or financial abuse.

55. Gently probe the client for an emotional reaction to being an abuse victim.

56. Facilitate the client in making changes of residence, program, or other contacts to terminate the abuse immediately.

57. Educate the client and caregivers about definitions of elder abuse, and how to report concerns to the clinician or local adult protective services unit.

58. Follow applicable abuse reporting procedures as outlined in local law and agency guidelines.

59. Advocate for the client to change his/her legal guardian or payee procedures to stem financial abuse.

60. Investigate spiritual concerns with the client, allowing the client to identify the relative importance of such issues for him/her.

61. Discuss with the client the potency of religious issues, and assist him/her in differentiating between religiously oriented mental illness symptoms (e.g., manic delusions about self or God) and legitimate religious issues.

62. Refer the client to a clergyperson who is knowledge-

able about aging and mental illness concerns.

63. Talk openly with the client about the specialized needs that he/she will face due to the natural deterioration of physical capabilities that are associated with aging.

64. Coordinate tours and other means of providing information regarding residential or other programs that are available for the client as he/she ages.

65. Assist the client in developing a written plan should he/she become legally unable to make his/her own decisions, including a plan for guardianship, advanced medical directives, and a last will and testament.

___. _____
_____

___. _____
_____

___. _____
_____

DIAGNOSTIC SUGGESTIONS

Axis I:	290.xx	Dementia of the Alzheimer's Type
	294.x	Dementia Due to . . . [General Medical Condition]
	297.1	Delusional Disorder
	295.xx	Schizophrenia
	295.10	Schizophrenia, Disorganized Type
	295.30	Schizophrenia, Paranoid Type
	295.90	Schizophrenia, Undifferentiated Type
	295.60	Schizophrenia, Residual Type

295.70	Schizoaffective Disorder
296.xx	Bipolar I Disorder
296.89	Bipolar II Disorder
780.9	Age-Related Cognitive Decline
_____	_____
_____	_____

ANGER MANAGEMENT

BEHAVIORAL DEFINITIONS

1. History of explosive, aggressive outbursts, out of proportion to any precipitating stressors, leading to assaultive acts or destruction of property.
2. Violent actions committed as a result of an altered perception of reality, such as hallucinations or delusions.
3. Impulsive anger outbursts due to a loss of natural inhibition, without regard to painful consequences.
4. Overreaction of hostility to insignificant irritants.
5. Paranoid ideation leading to easily feeling offended, quick anger responses, and defensive behaviors.
6. Violent actions, threats, or verbally abusive language used to intimidate or control others when feeling threatened.
7. Consistent pattern of disrespectful treatment of or challenging authority figures.
8. Body language of tense muscles (e.g., clenched fist or jaw, glaring looks, or refusal to make eye contact).
9. A history of being verbally, physically, or sexually abused, resulting in overreactions to natural stressors.
10. Self-directed anger, as evidenced by self-mutilating behavior or suicide threats or attempts.

—. _____
   _____
   _____
—. _____
   _____
   _____
—. _____
   _____

LONG-TERM GOALS

1. Decrease in overall intensity of angry feelings and an increase in the ability to recognize and respectfully express angry feelings.
2. Maintain reality orientation to decrease angry psychotic outbursts.
3. Increase natural inhibitions by stabilizing thought disorder.
4. Increase stress management skills to reduce irritability.
5. Develop and maintain relationships based on realistic level of trust.
6. Increase relationship skills such as assertiveness, communicating feelings, or compromise to get needs met.
7. Maintain healthy respect for others, including personal space, property, and basic human rights.
8. Develop safety skills to decrease fears of abuse.
9. Discontinue self-directed harmful behaviors.

—. _____
_____
—. _____
_____
—. _____
_____

SHORT-TERM OBJECTIVES

1. Describe the history of anger management problems. (1, 2, 3, 4)
2. Identify current anger control challenges. (4, 5, 6, 7)
3. Identify the relationship between mental illness symptoms and anger control problems. (8, 9)
4. Gain admission to a safe and controlled environment. (10, 11)
5. Acknowledge the presence of thoughts, feelings, or

THERAPEUTIC INTERVENTIONS

1. Focus on developing a level of trust with the client. Provide support and empathy to encourage the client to feel safe in expressing his/her angry emotions.
2. Request the client to identify his/her history of anger management problems including lost relationships, legal problems, or outbursts.
3. Utilize a graphic display such as a timeline to help the client identify the pattern of anger problems that

urges to direct anger at self. (10, 11, 12)

6. Obtain a complete physical evaluation to rule out medical etiologies for anger outbursts. (13, 14)

7. Acknowledge the abuse of alcohol or street drugs and its relationship to anger mismanagement. (15)

8. Terminate the abuse of alcohol and/or street drugs. (16)

9. Cooperate with a referral to a physician for medication evaluation. (17)

10. Report a decrease in anger-producing mental illness symptoms through the regular use of psychotropic medications. (17, 18, 19)

11. Report the side effects and effectiveness of medications to the appropriate professional. (18, 19, 20)

12. Attend individual and/or group therapy sessions that are focused on anger management. (21)

13. Identify triggers and causes for anger outbursts. (6, 8, 21, 22)

14. Identify the pain, hurt, and other emotions that prompt anger. (1, 21, 23, 24)

15. Identify how anger expression has been modeled by others in the past. (7, 21, 25)

16. Maintain reality orientation. (17, 26, 28)

he/she has revealed (e.g., when they started, how they have varied in intensity or type over time, the consequences, etc.).

4. Coordinate psychological testing to assess the extent and severity of the client's anger management problems.

5. Question the client about current functioning regarding anger management.

6. Provide the client, family, or caretaker with an anger journal or log to track frequency, intensity, duration, and consequences of anger expression difficulties.

7. Assign the client to read portions of Rosellini and Worden's *Of Course You're Angry* or *The Angry Book* by Rubin; process the application of the content to his/her experience.

8. Request that the client identify the hallucinations or delusions that he/she has experienced (currently or in the past) and how these internal stimuli have prompted anger outbursts (e.g., delusional fear prompting defensive anger).

9. Expand the client's understanding of the issues of loss of control due to severe and persistent mental illness symptoms and the attempt to regain control through temper outbursts.

17. Differentiate between paranoid ideation and legitimate anger triggers. (6, 8, 27, 28)
18. Verbally express angry emotions in a controlled, assertive, safe manner. (21, 29, 30, 31)
19. Express emotions in nonverbal ways. (31, 32, 33)
20. Utilize relaxation techniques to cope with angry feelings. (21, 34)
21. Identify the negative impact of anger outbursts on others. (3, 6, 35, 36)
22. Learn and implement improved social skills. (37, 38)
23. Delay reactions long enough to consider the consequences of an angry outburst. (17, 30, 33, 39)
24. Verbalize the intense feelings that motivate self-mutilating behavior and how these feelings are relieved by such behavior. (21, 23, 40, 41)
25. Develop a plan for safely expressing appropriate anger to the perpetrator of abuse. (21, 42, 43, 44)
26. Identify the effects of holding on to anger. (21, 45, 46)
27. Report success at moving past anger and toward forgiveness. (21, 33, 46, 47, 48)
28. Family, friends, and caregivers learn techniques to assist the client's anger management endeavors. (49, 50, 51)

10. Arrange for admission into a crisis residential unit or psychiatric hospital if the client is judged to be an imminent risk of harm to himself/herself or others.
11. Remove anger-provoking stimuli (e.g., antagonistic peer, persistent noises, noxious smells) from the client's environment.
12. Assess the client for the potential of directing anger at himself/herself, resulting in self-harm or a suicide attempt.
13. Refer the client to a general physician for a complete physical examination to rule out medical etiologies for anger outbursts.
14. Assist the client in following up on recommendations from the physical evaluation such as specialty assessments, lab work, or medications.
15. Review the client's use of street drugs or alcohol as a contributing factor to anger control problems.
16. Conduct or refer the client for substance abuse evaluation and treatment. (See the Chemical Dependence chapter in this Planner.)
17. Refer the client to a physician for an evaluation as to the need for psychotropic medications.
18. Educate the client about the use and expected benefits of medication.

29. Respond to and complete the mandates of the court relative to legal charges resulting from anger management problems. (52, 53, 54)

—. _____
   _____

—. _____
   _____

—. _____
   _____

19. Monitor the client's medication compliance and effectiveness.

20. Review the side effects of the medications with the client and the medical staff to identify possible side effects or confounding influence of polypharmacy.

21. Refer the client to a therapist who specializes in the treatment of the severely and persistently mentally ill for individual or group treatment of anger control problems.

22. Request that the client develop a list of all situations, events, people, and so on, that cause anger, irritation, or disappointment. Review the list and prompt the client about areas that seem to be missing.

23. Assist the client in naming emotions (e.g., anger, hurt, shame, etc.) that underlie his/her cycle of anger. Utilize pictorial displays of emotions to help the client identify hard-to-name emotions.

24. Emphasize to the client the variety of social cues that can assist in identifying emotions in self and others (e.g., context, body language, etc.).

25. Assist the client in identifying positive and negative ways in which key life figures have expressed angry feelings and how these ex-

periences have influenced the client's pattern of anger management.

26. Assist the client in focusing on reality rather than on hallucinations or delusions. (See the Psychosis chapter in this Planner.)

27. Request that the client identify specific instances of paranoid ideation that have contributed to angry outbursts.

28. Request that the client identify a few trusted individuals to whom he/she can turn for reality testing.

29. Conduct or refer the client for assertiveness training.

30. Review recent temper outbursts, focusing on alternative ways in which those emotions could have been expressed.

31. Utilize role playing, modeling, and behavior rehearsal to teach the client nonaggressive ways of handling angry feelings.

32. Educate the client on how to use his/her body language to communicate emotions accurately.

33. Reinforce the client's use of alternative, healthy techniques for managing angry feelings.

34. Teach the client deep muscle relaxation and deep breathing techniques (e.g., see *The Relaxation and Stress Reduction Workbook*

by Davis, Eshelman, and McKay).

35. Request that the client obtain specific feedback from loved ones about how his/her anger has affected them.

36. Process the effects of anger outbursts with the client. Present a variety of reactions that others may experience toward the client's anger.

37. Teach the client social skills (e.g., eye contact, conversation, showing interest in others) that are necessary to improve social relationships. (See the Social Skills chapter in this Planner.)

38. Refer the client to a support group for individuals with severe and persistent mental illness.

39. Teach the client to utilize thought-stopping techniques to slow anger reactions (e.g., see *The Depression Workbook* by Copeland).

40. Explore the client's history of self-harm and interpret the self-mutilating behaviors as an expression of the rage and helplessness that he/she has not been able to express toward the appropriate target.

41. Help the client develop a safety plan (e.g., call a friend, contact a crisis line, go to a public area) for situ-

ations in which the client experiences the urge to engage in self-mutilating behaviors.

42. Direct the client to write a letter to the perpetrator of abuse about how his/her abusive actions have behaviorally affected the client and the emotions that are related to that abuse.

43. Role-play possible scenarios for expressing anger directly to the perpetrator of abuse and the possible outcomes.

44. Thoroughly review the emotional and physical safety needs that the client may have regarding the direct expression of anger to a perpetrator of abuse. Offer to attend the meeting to provide support to the client, if appropriate.

45. Discuss the effects of maintaining anger, including both positive (e.g., increased vigilance to abuse) and negative (e.g., bitterness, outbursts).

46. Assign the client to read *Forgive and Forget* (Smedes); process key ideas with the client.

47. Ask the client to write a forgiving letter to the target of the anger; process with the client the content of the letter and whether it should be sent.

48. Refer the client to a pastor, rabbi, priest, or other cleric

to help process the spiritual need for forgiveness.

49. Educate family, friends, and caregivers about the symptoms of mental illness, emphasizing the nonvolitional aspects of some symptoms.

50. Develop a safety plan with family, friends, and caregivers, focusing on how to manage these anger episodes, and at what point to contact public safety officials. Educate the client about the safety plan.

51. Role-play with the client's family, friends, and caregivers the assertive, safe, direct responses to the client's anger outbursts.

52. With the proper release of information, provide the court with information about the client's mental illness symptoms and treatment.

53. Advocate within the court system for the client to receive assistance, representation, leniency, or sentencing that is commensurate with his/her mental illness concerns.

54. Assist the client in meeting a court-mandated sentence by coordinating transportation, community service, or assisting the client in communicating with court officials. (See the Legal Concerns chapter in this Planner.)

—. _____
    _____
    _____

—. _____
    _____
    _____

—. _____
    _____
    _____

DIAGNOSTIC SUGGESTIONS

Axis I:
297.1	Delusional Disorder
295.xx	Schizophrenia
295.0	Schizophrenia, Disorganized Type
295.70	Schizoaffective Disorder
296.xx	Bipolar I Disorder
296.89	Bipolar II Disorder
312.43	Intermittent Explosive Disorder
312.8	Conduct Disorder
310.1	Personality Change Due to . . . [Axis III Disorder]
309.81	Posttraumatic Stress Disorder
V61.9	Relational Problem Related to a Mental Disorder
V62.81	Relational Problem NOS
_____	_____
_____	_____

Axis II:
301.83	Borderline Personality Disorder
301.7	Antisocial Personality Disorder
301.0	Paranoid Personality Disorder
301.81	Narcissistic Personality Disorder
301.9	Personality Disorder NOS
_____	_____
_____	_____

ANXIETY

BEHAVIORAL DEFINITIONS

1. Apprehension in response to severe and persistent mental illness symptoms (e.g., frightening hallucinations or manic/racing thoughts).
2. Excessive and persistent daily worry about life circumstances that has no factual or logical basis.
3. Motor tension such as restlessness, tiredness, shakiness, or muscle tautness.
4. Recurrent or persistent fear due to persecutory delusions or other bizarre beliefs.
5. Hypervigilance as indicated by constantly feeling on edge, difficulty sleeping, or irritability.
6. Concentration difficulties, such as losing a train of thought or forgetfulness, related to anxious preoccupation.
7. Panic attacks as evidenced by discrete, brief periods of intense fear and discomfort.
8. Obsessive thoughts and/or compulsive behaviors in an attempt to decrease a sense of fear.
9. Persistent and unreasonable fear of a specific object or situation resulting in avoidance of that object or situation.

—. _____

_____

_____

—. _____

_____

_____

—. _____

_____

LONG-TERM GOALS

1. Decrease internal stimuli that contribute to feelings of anxiety.
2. Resolve anxiety related to severe and persistent mental illness symptoms.
3. Decrease the level of worry, anxiety, panic, obsessions, or compulsions.
4. Manage normal life stressors with minimal levels of anxiety.
5. Learn coping techniques to decrease the effects of anxiety.
6. Increase concentration and ability to function on a daily basis.
7. Resolve core conflicts that are the source of the anxiety.

—. _____
   _____
   _____
—. _____
   _____
   _____
—. _____
   _____

SHORT-TERM OBJECTIVES

1. Describe the history of anxiety symptoms. (1, 2, 3, 4)
2. Differentiate between symptoms that are related to anxiety versus those that are related to severe and persistent mental illness. (2, 4, 5, 6)
3. Verbalize an understanding of the cognitive etiology of anxiety symptoms. (5, 7, 8)
4. Identify a secondary gain that may be reinforcing anxiety symptoms. (9)
5. Identify key life conflicts that raise anxiety. (10, 11, 12)
6. Take steps to reduce external sources of stress. (13)

THERAPEUTIC INTERVENTIONS

1. Focus on developing a level of trust with the client. Provide support and empathy to encourage the client to feel safe in expressing his/her anxiety symptoms.
2. Request the client to describe his/her history of anxiety symptoms, including phobias, panic attacks, generalized anxiety, obsessions, or compulsions.
3. Utilize a graphic display, such as a timeline, to help the client identify the pattern of anxiety symptoms that he/she has experienced (e.g., when they started, how they have varied in intensity or type over time).

7. Implement cognitive and behavioral coping techniques to reduce anxiety. (14, 15, 16, 17, 50)

8. Obtain a complete physical evaluation to rule out medical etiologies for anxiety symptoms. (18, 19)

9. Identify any foods, alcohol, or street drugs that could be triggering anxiety. (20, 21)

10. Cooperate with a medication evaluation. (22)

11. Report a decrease in anxiety symptoms through regular use of psychotropic medications. (22, 23, 24)

12. Report the side effects and effectiveness of the medications to the appropriate professional. (24, 25)

13. Attend individual and/or group therapy sessions that are focused on anxiety reduction. (26)

14. Apply stress reduction techniques to severe mental illness symptoms. (14, 15, 16, 27)

15. Implement a quieter, more routine environment. (28, 29, 30)

16. Divert attention away from anxiety and toward other activities. (31, 36)

17. Significant others should encourage the client in implementing stress reduction techniques. (32, 47)

18. Implement cognitive and behavioral techniques to de-

4. Coordinate psychological testing to assess the extent and severity of anxiety symptoms.

5. Utilizing a description of anxiety symptoms such as that found in Bourne's *The Anxiety and Phobia Workbook,* help the client to identify with a specific diagnostic classification.

6. Help the client differentiate symptoms that are a direct effect of his/her severe and persistent mental illness, as opposed to a separate diagnosis of an anxiety disorder.

7. Provide the client with specific information regarding the cognitive precursors of anxiety (e.g., *Anxiety Disorders and Phobias: A Cognitive Perspective* by Beck).

8. Help the client to apply the cognitive etiology information to his/her specific symptoms and experience of anxiety.

9. Assist the client in identifying a secondary gain that is achieved by the presence of the anxiety symptoms (e.g., lowered expectations from others).

10. Explore the client's life for circumstances that may induce anxiety.

11. Assist the client in differentiating between actual life situations and those that appear real, but are due to hallucinations or delusions.

crease the intensity, duration, and frequency of panic attacks. (33, 34, 35)

19. Increase daily social and vocational involvement. (36, 37)

20. Identify and replace dysfunctional beliefs that maintain anxiety. (38, 39, 40, 50)

21. Interrupt obsessions with thought-stopping techniques. (26, 41)

22. Reduce the time involved and interference from obsessions and compulsions. (26, 42, 43, 44)

23. Resolve traumatic incidents from the past, decreasing hypervigilance, nightmares, flashbacks, or distress. (1, 26, 45, 46)

24. Contact supportive people when anxiety symptoms are severe. (32, 47, 48)

25. Attend a self-help group for support. (49)

26. Utilize positive self-talk techniques to decrease anxiety and raise self-esteem. (50, 51)

27. Take increased control over own needs. (31, 52)

__. _____
   _____

__. _____
   _____

__. _____
   _____

12. Acknowledge that both real and delusional experiences can cause anxiety, providing support to the client.

13. Participate with the client in developing plans for resolving identifiable external stressors (e.g., housing, financial, medical treatment, etc.). Facilitate resolution in this area that the client is unable to resolve on his/her own.

14. Encourage the client to take a prominent role in identifying specific techniques that have had a reducing effect on his/her anxiety symptoms in the past; direct the client to implement these previously successful measures more consistently.

15. Train the client in guided imagery techniques (e.g., identifying several characteristics of a quiet, serene place, or "surfing a panic attack").

16. Teach the client deep muscle relaxation and deep breathing to reduce anxiety symptoms; utilize biofeedback techniques to facilitate relaxation skills.

17. Direct the client to choose an applicable chapter from *The Relaxation and Stress Reduction Workbook* by Davis, Eshelman, and McKay, then support the client in implementing the chosen techniques.

18. Refer the client to a general physician for a complete physical examination to evaluate for any organic basis for the anxiety.

19. Assist the client in following up on the recommendations from a physical evaluation, including medications, lab work, or specialty assessments.

20. Review the client's use of psychoactive chemicals (e.g., nicotine, caffeine, alcohol abuse, or street drugs) and their relationship to symptoms.

21. Recommend the termination of consumption of substances that could trigger anxiety; refer for substance abuse evaluation or treatment if indicated.

22. Refer the client to a physician for an evaluation as to the need for psychotropic medications.

23. Educate the client about the use and expected benefits of the medication.

24. Monitor the client's medication compliance and effectiveness; reinforce consistent use of the medication.

25. Review the effects of the medications with the client and the medical staff to identify possible side effects or confounding influence of polypharmacy.

26. Refer the client to a therapist for individual or group

therapy regarding anxiety symptoms.

27. Request that the client identify ways in which stress reduction techniques can be applied to other severe and persistent mental illness symptoms.

28. Help the client to modify his/her environment to be more soothing (e.g., soft lighting, low music, comfortable temperature).

29. Encourage the client to develop a routine daily pattern, including waking and resting at the same times, establishing regular mealtimes, and routinely performing daily chores.

30. Teach the client how a calm environment and predictable, regular routine help to decrease anxiety.

31. Assist the client in identifying a list of alternative diversionary activities to utilize when experiencing anxiety (e.g., taking a walk, watching TV or video, doing a household chore, calling a friend or family member, etc.).

32. Enlist the help of the client's support system in implementing specific stress reduction techniques.

33. Help the client to identify that although the panic attack is terrifying, it is by nature short term, pre-

dictable, and relatively harmless when completed.

34. Request that the client identify realistic, positive responses to frightening thoughts that he/she has experienced during panic attacks. Direct the client to write these on a set of 3-by-5-inch cards and to refer to them when experiencing a panic attack.

35. Utilize role playing, modeling, and behavior rehearsal to encourage the client to use breathing and muscle relaxation techniques to help work through a panic attack and to induce relaxation.

36. Assist the client in identifying appropriate and available community-based social, vocational, or recreational programs or activities in which he/she could become involved.

37. Utilize systematic desensitization techniques to help the client gradually to decrease anxiety that leads to avoidance and to increase his/her involvement in the community.

38. Request that the client identify beliefs that support the anxiety. Help the client to question these beliefs and to identify healthier, more realistic beliefs in this area.

39. Help the client to identify and label psychotic or delusional beliefs, and to develop coping skills for such. (See the Psychosis chapter in this Planner.)

40. Analyze the fear with the patient by examining the probability of the negative expectation that is occurring, what will be the real impact if it does occur, his/her ability to control it, as well as his/her ability to accept it. (See *Anxiety Disorders and Phobias* by Beck.)

41. Assign thought-stopping techniques that interfere cognitively with obsession (i.e., visualize a stop sign, then a serene visual image, or snap a rubber band on the wrist to stop the dysfunctional thought).

42. Associate a negative situation (e.g., a necessary but unpleasant task) with the obsession or compulsion by requiring that the client engage in the negative behavior when experiencing the obsession or compulsion.

43. Replace the obsession or compulsion with a less intensive and less intrusive behavior or thought by asking the client to identify a less intrusive replacement ritual.

44. Use Rational Emotive Therapy techniques to analyze, refute, and replace self-defeating beliefs.

45. Request that the client identify traumatic experiences and their associated feelings in a safe, nonjudgmental atmosphere.

46. Engage in a ritual to provide closure to a traumatic incident (e.g., writing emotions on paper, then ripping them up, and tossing them into the wind).

47. With the proper release of information, provide feedback to the client's support system about his/her symptoms and how to help him/her manage them.

48. Encourage the client to identify support people with whom he/she has had positive experiences. Encourage the client to utilize these people for reality testing and support.

49. Refer the client to a self-help support group for anxiety disorders or chronic mental illness symptoms.

50. Assess the client's ability to tolerate the use of self-talk techniques (e.g., understand the difference between self-talk and auditory hallucinations).

51. Teach the client self-talk techniques such as those described in Bourne's *The Anxiety and Phobia Workbook*.

52. Encourage the client to take responsibility for his/her personal needs wherever possible (e.g., cooking

his/her own meals, managing all or part of his/her financial needs).

—. _____
   _____
   _____
—. _____
   _____
—. _____
   _____

DIAGNOSTIC SUGGESTIONS

Axis I:	297.1	Delusional Disorder
	295.xx	Schizophrenia
	295.10	Schizophrenia, Disorganized Type
	295.20	Schizophrenia, Catatonic Type
	295.90	Schizophrenia, Undifferentiated Type
	295.30	Schizophrenia, Paranoid Type
	295.70	Schizoaffective Disorder
	296.xx	Bipolar I Disorder
	296.89	Bipolar II Disorder
	298.9	Psychotic Disorder NOS
	300.01	Panic Disorder Without Agoraphobia
	300.21	Panic Disorder With Agoraphobia
	300.22	Agoraphobia Without History of Panic Disorder
	300.29	Specific Phobia
	300.23	Social Phobia
	300.3	Obsessive-Compulsive Disorder
	309.81	Posttraumatic Stress Disorder
	300.02	Generalized Anxiety Disorder
	293.89	Anxiety Disorder Due to . . . [Axis III Disorder]
	_____	_____
	_____	_____
Axis II:	301.4	Obsessive-Compulsive Personality Disorder
	_____	_____
	_____	_____

CHEMICAL DEPENDENCE

BEHAVIORAL DEFINITIONS

1. Consistent use of alcohol or other mood-altering substances (not including prescribed medications) until high, intoxicated, or passed out.
2. Exacerbation of primary (e.g., hallucinations, delusions, mania) or secondary (e.g., anxiety, unstable affect, disorganization) psychosis symptoms as a result of the use of or withdrawal from mood-altering illicit substances.
3. Inability to stop or cut down on the use of mood-altering substances once started, despite the verbalized desire to do so or the negative consequences that continued use brings.
4. Blood tests reflecting a pattern of heavy substance abuse (for example, elevated liver enzymes).
5. Denial that chemical dependence is a problem, despite direct feedback from family, peers, or treatment staff that the substance use is negatively affecting the client's functioning or relationships.
6. Continued drug and/or alcohol use despite experiencing persistent or recurring physical, legal, vocational, social, or relationship problems that are directly caused by the use of the substance.
7. Diversion of limited financial or personal resources into obtaining the substance, using the substance, or recovering from the effects of the substance.
8. Use of substances despite medical warnings from a physician about the interactions of psychotropic medications and illicit substances.
9. Gradual increase in the consumption of the mood-altering substance in larger amounts and for longer periods than intended to obtain the desired effect.
10. Physical symptoms, including shaking, seizures, nausea, headaches, sweating, or insomnia, when withdrawing from the substance.

11. Relapse into abuse of mood-altering substances after substantial period of sobriety.

___. _____

_____

___. _____

_____

___. _____

_____

LONG-TERM GOALS

1. Accept the chemical dependence and begin to actively participate in an integrated, dual-diagnosis recovery program.
2. Withdraw from mood-altering substance; stabilize physically, emotionally, and psychiatrically; and then establish a supportive recovery plan.
3. Gain an understanding of the negative impact of substance use on psychiatric symptoms and the effectiveness of psychotropic medications.
4. Establish a sustained recovery, free from the use of illicit mood-altering substances.
5. Establish and maintain total abstinence while increasing knowledge of the disease, interaction with mental illness concerns, and the process of an integrated recovery.
6. Acquire the necessary skills to maintain a long-term sobriety from all illicit mood-altering substances.
7. Improve the quality of life by maintaining an ongoing abstinence from all illicit mood-altering substances.
8. Develop an understanding of a personal pattern of relapse to help sustain long-term recovery.
9. Contribute personal resources, including an understanding of the unique role of mental illness in recovery issues, to aid in the recovery of others.

___. _____

_____

___. _____

_____

___. _____

_____

SHORT-TERM OBJECTIVES

1. Achieve a medically safe detoxification from substances. (1, 2, 3, 4, 5)

2. Achieve normal orientation and perceptions. (4, 6, 7)

3. Identify and accept the need for substance abuse treatment. (8, 9, 10)

4. Improve medical stability relative to the effects of long-term substance abuse. (11, 12)

5. Improve nutritional/dietary status relative to the effects of long-term substance abuse. (13, 14)

6. Maintain or acquire adequate, safe housing or residential placement. (15, 16, 17)

7. Accept the legal consequences of behavior related to substance abuse. (18, 19, 20)

8. Identify recent experiences of victimization relative to a compromised mental condition due to chronic substance abuse. (21, 22)

9. Describe the amount, frequency, and history of substance abuse. (23, 24, 25, 26)

10. Identify the benefits that promote substance abuse, including the effect on mental illness symptoms. (27)

11. Identify the negative consequences of substance abuse,

THERAPEUTIC INTERVENTIONS

1. Obtain permission from the client to remove available substances from his/her immediate access.

2. Refer the client to an emergency room for immediate medical assessment/care relative to present substance use and intoxication.

3. Assess the client's current level of intoxication by a subjective means, such as reviewing behavior or speech, or by an objective means, such as obtaining a Breathalyzer.

4. Refer the client to an acute detoxification unit in a substance abuse treatment program.

5. Assess the client's suicide risk, providing for or coordinating constant supervision, if needed.

6. Reorient the client to person, place, and time.

7. Provide simple, basic directions to focus the client on meeting his/her basic needs for safety and on decreasing the mood-altering effects of substances.

8. Help the client identify history and effects of substance abuse, including the inability to control substance abuse.

9. Coordinate family members, friends, and colleagues

including the exacerbation of mental illness symptoms. (28, 29)

12. Identify realistic goals for substance abuse recovery. (30, 31, 32)

13. Decrease the frequency of substance use and the quantity used. (33, 34, 35)

14. Take psychotropic medications as prescribed. (36, 37, 38)

15. Report the side effects and the effectiveness of the medications to an appropriate professional. (37, 38, 39)

16. Report positive effects of the medications on the perceived need for substances. (36, 37, 40)

17. Acknowledge the negative effects of substance abuse on health and housing and accept assistance in resolving these problems. (16, 17, 41)

18. Verbalize an understanding of the effects of substance abuse on the mind and body. (42)

19. Identify triggers that are related to the use of substances. (43, 44)

20. Accept responsibility for behavior and acknowledge the relationship between personal problems, exacerbated mental illness symptoms, and substance abuse. (19, 42, 45, 46)

21. Identify current family and peer conflicts that con-

to confront the client about the negative effects that substance abuse has had on their lives and on their relationships with the client.

10. Assign chapters from *The 12 Steps—A Way Out* by Friends in Recovery.

11. Encourage the client to maintain ADLs.

12. Refer to medical staff, such as an agency nurse or a personal physician, to assess the client's physical/medical needs.

13. Encourage the client to maintain healthy nutrition.

14. Refer to a dietitian or a nutritionist for an assessment or recommendations regarding the client's dietary needs.

15. Assist the client in identifying residential needs.

16. Coordinate obtaining crisis housing, as needed.

17. Facilitate an agreement between the client and the landlord or home provider regarding expectations for the client to remain in a residential situation that has been compromised due to his/her exacerbated psychiatric symptoms and substance abuse.

18. With proper release, provide information to police/prosecutor regarding the impact of the client's mental illness on his/her behavior.

tribute to substance abuse. (47, 48)

22. Identify and verbalize feelings to promote stress relief and to increase communication. (49, 50, 51)

23. Practice and implement relaxation skills. (52)

24. Verbalize positive feelings toward self. (53, 54, 55, 56)

25. Practice improved social skills and implement them in increased social contacts. (57, 58, 59)

26. Structure time and increase self-esteem by obtaining employment. (60, 61)

27. Verbalize a sense of hope and fulfilled spiritual needs. (55, 59, 62, 63)

28. Ask family, friends, and an AA/NA sponsor to support sobriety. (59, 64, 65)

29. Verbally identify the specific symptoms, behaviors, or beliefs that have led to substance use/relapse, focusing on the triggers for relapse. (66, 67)

30. Family members increase positive support of the client to reduce stress, support sobriety, and decrease exacerbation of the primary symptoms. (68, 69, 70, 71, 72)

31. Attend a 12-step program consistently to support and maintain sobriety. (59, 62, 65, 73)

19. Urge the client to accept personal responsibility for substance abuse and consequent erratic behavior.

20. Facilitate the client's involvement with legal appointments, court dates, and so forth.

21. Ask the client about any recent history of having experienced sexual, physical, or other types of victimization, providing empathetic support regarding possible abuse.

22. Contact adult protective services staff regarding abuse to individuals who are unable to advocate for themselves.

23. Gather a complete drug/alcohol history, including the amount and the pattern of use.

24. Request that family, peers, and other treatment staff provide additional information regarding the client's substance use history.

25. Administer the Alcohol Severity Index and process the findings with the client.

26. Refer to a substance abuse agency that is knowledgeable about mental illness issues for a substance abuse assessment.

27. Request that the client make a list of reasons why substance use is attractive (i.e., self-medication of psychotic and other severe

32. Accept the long-term nature of substance abuse problems, mental illness, and the need for ongoing treatment. (32, 40, 42, 73, 74)

—. _____
   _____

—. _____
   _____

—. _____
   _____

mental illness symptoms, novelty seeking), and process this with the clinician.

28. Ask the client to make a list of negative ways in which substances have affected his/her life, and process it with the clinician.

29. Assign the client to ask two or three people who are close to him/her to write a letter describing how the substance abuse has affected them, and process it with the clinician.

30. Request that the client write out basic expectations (e.g., physical changes, social changes, emotional needs) regarding sobriety, and process these with the clinician.

31. Continue to focus on the need for substance abuse recovery and on the need for sobriety, despite relapses.

32. Plan for an extended monitoring of the chronic nature and high recidivism of mentally ill substance abusers.

33. Request that the client chart his/her substance use for a designated period of time, and process it with the clinician.

34. Ask the client to identify two trigger situations in which he/she has successfully decreased or declined substance use.

35. Process ways in which the client was successful in de-

creasing or declining substance use, and how to generalize these successes in other areas.

36. Arrange for a psychiatric evaluation by a physician who is familiar with substance abuse issues to assess the need for psychotropic medications, or Antabuse.

37. Educate the client about the use of and the expected benefits of medications.

38. Monitor the client's medication compliance and effectiveness.

39. Review the side effects of the medication with the client and medical staff to determine the possible impact of the side effects as a trigger to substance use.

40. Educate the client about the expected or common psychiatric symptoms of his/her mental illness, which impact upon substance use and abuse.

41. Refer the client for a medical evaluation regarding possible physical problems that are related to a chronic history of substance abuse.

42. Provide factual information about the effects of substance abuse on physical and mental health.

43. Request that the client identify feelings, behaviors, and situations that place

him/her at a higher risk for substance abuse.

44. Request that the client identify specific primary psychotic symptoms that effect the desire for substances.

45. Confront the use of defense mechanisms to justify or rationalize behavior.

46. Reinforce the client for taking responsibility for his/her substance abuse behavior and for committing to a plan of recovery.

47. Request that the client identify the ways in which family and peer conflicts have contributed to his/her stress level, increasing the likelihood to react with substance abuse.

48. Refer the client for family therapy regarding interpersonal conflicts and effects of mental illness on the family members.

49. Encourage verbalizing emotions, focusing on fears and anxiety-producing situations.

50. Assist the client in identifying feelings regarding substance use and abuse, including anger and helplessness.

51. Assign the client to read chapters from *Of Course You're Angry* by Rosselini and Worden.

52. Teach the client relaxation techniques, such as progres-

sive muscle relaxation or safe-place visualization.

53. Build the client's self-esteem through verbalizing an acceptance of him/her in spite of his/her mental illness.

54. Encourage the client to explore new areas to develop skills and abilities, such as hobbies or volunteer work.

55. Teach the client the use of positive self-affirmations.

56. Refer the client to individual or group therapy, focusing on self-esteem issues.

57. Practice a variety of social skills with the client. (See the Social Skills chapter in this Planner.)

58. Refer to drop-in centers, clubhouse programs, and community-based social programs.

59. Refer the client to Alcoholics Anonymous (AA) or Narcotics Anonymous (NA), or AA/NA for dual-diagnosis clients.

60. Coach the client on preparing for employment, searching for a job, and maintaining employment. (See the Employment Problems chapter in this Planner.)

61. Refer the client to supported employment program.

62. Provide basic information on the 12-step program and philosophy, such as *The*

Twelve Steps for Everyone . . . Who Really Wants Them by Grateful Members.

63. Refer the client to a cleric regarding spiritual questions and needs.

64. Encourage the client to solicit family support for his/her sober lifestyle.

65. Coordinate a sponsor from a 12-step program, providing additional information to the sponsor regarding mental illness issues.

66. Assign portions of *The Addiction Workbook* by Fanning and O'Neill to help the client identify triggers for relapse.

67. Ask the client to develop a list of symptoms, behaviors, and beliefs that could have been involved in the relapse, and then develop adaptive strategies to overcome those triggers.

68. With the proper release of information, answer family questions about the client's mental illness symptoms, and the interaction of symptoms and substances.

69. Refer the family members to a community-based support group for loved ones of a chronically, mentally ill substance abuser.

70. Encourage family members to identify and vent about the client's past behavior and symptoms.

71. Coordinate a family therapy session to allow the family to express their concerns, emotions, and expectations directly to the client.

72. Refer family members to read *Codependent No More* by Beattie.

73. Encourage and reinforce consistent attendance at 12-step recovery program meetings three or more times per week.

74. Coordinate a contact between the client and another mentally ill individual who is further along in substance abuse recovery (e.g., three years or more) to process how he/she has achieved this success.

—. _____
   _____
—. _____
   _____
—. _____
   _____

DIAGNOSTIC SUGGESTIONS

Axis I:	303.90	Alcohol Dependence
	305.00	Alcohol Abuse
	304.30	Cannabis Dependence
	305.20	Cannabis Abuse
	304.20	Cocaine Dependence
	305.60	Cocaine Abuse
	304.80	Polysubstance Dependence
	297.1	Delusional Disorder
	295.xx	Schizophrenia
	295.10	Schizophrenia, Disorganized Type

295.30	Schizophrenia, Paranoid Type
295.70	Schizoaffective Disorder
296.xx	Bipolar I Disorder
296.89	Bipolar II Disorder
_____	_____
_____	_____

DEPRESSION

BEHAVIORAL DEFINITIONS

1. Changes in appetite.
2. Depressed affect.
3. Diminished interest in or pleasure derived from previously enjoyable activities.
4. Sleeplessness or hypersomnia.
5. Decreased energy level.
6. Chronic feelings of hopelessness, worthlessness, or inappropriate guilt.
7. Hallucinations or delusions secondary to and congruent with depressed mood.
8. Multiple losses related to severe and persistent mental illness symptoms resulting in sorrow, grief, or despair.
9. Suicidal ideation, statements, gestures, or attempts.
10. Low self-esteem.

___. _____
    _____
    _____
___. _____
    _____
___. _____
    _____

LONG-TERM GOALS

1. Alleviate depressed mood and return to premorbid level of functioning.
2. Maintain reality orientation, no longer experiencing thought disturbance that is related to depression.

3. Recognize, accept, and cope with indicators of depression.
4. Accept losses and develop positive self-esteem that is based on personal strengths.
5. Stabilize appetite, sleep pattern, and energy level.
6. Develop increased involvement in personal interests.
7. Express emotions regarding losses that are related to severe and persistent mental illness symptoms.
8. Assure safety regarding suicidal impulses.

—. _____
   _____
   _____
—. _____
   _____
   _____
—. _____
   _____

SHORT-TERM OBJECTIVES

1. Describe the history of depression symptoms. (1, 2, 3)

2. Identify the current depression symptoms. (4, 5, 6)

3. Cooperate with suicide prevention measures. (4, 7, 8)

4. Obtain a complete physical evaluation to rule out medical etiologies for depression symptoms. (9, 10, 11)

5. Acknowledge the abuse of alcohol and street drugs and their relationship to depression. (11, 12)

6. Cooperate with a referral to a physician for a psychotropic medication evaluation. (13)

7. Report a decrease in depression symptoms through the

THERAPEUTIC INTERVENTIONS

1. Request that the client identify his/her own, as well as the family's, history of depression symptoms.

2. Ask family, friends, and caregivers about the client's own and the family's history of depression symptoms.

3. Utilize a graphic display, such as a timeline, to help the client identify the pattern of his/her depression symptoms.

4. Question the client about current functioning regarding depression symptoms (e.g., mood/affect, sleep, appetite, suicidal thoughts, guilt, delusion, etc.).

5. Provide the client, family, or caretaker with sleeping,

regular use of psychiatric medications. (13, 14, 15)

8. Report the side effects and effectiveness of medications to the appropriate professional. (15, 16, 17)

9. Attend individual and/or group psychotherapy sessions focused on depression treatment. (18)

10. Verbally identify the source of the depressed mood. (18, 19, 20)

11. Experience the sadness that is related to past losses. (18, 20, 21, 22)

12. Identify specific losses that are related to severe and persistent mental illness symptoms. (18, 22, 23)

13. Verbalize an understanding of the general etiology and treatment of depression. (24, 25)

14. Verbally express an understanding of the relationship between a depressed mood and the repression of feelings (e.g., anger, hurt, and sadness). (21, 23, 26)

15. Express previously repressed emotions in a safe, cathartic manner. (27, 28)

16. Identify and replace cognitive self-talk that is engaged in to support depression. (29, 30, 31, 32)

17. Implement an assertive means of expressing anger. (33, 34, 46)

eating, and activity logs on which to document current levels of functioning.

6. Refer the client for psychological testing to assess the depth and signs of depression.

7. Coordinate an immediate referral to a crisis residential facility or inpatient psychiatric ward to provide safe, supervised environment for suicidal client.

8. Develop a structured suicide prevention plan. (See the Suicidal Ideation chapter in this Planner.)

9. Refer the client to a physician for a complete physical examination to rule out medical etiologies for depression.

10. Assist the client in following up on recommendations from physical evaluation including medications, lab work, or specialty assessments.

11. Review the client's use of stimulants (e.g., nicotine, caffeine, or street drugs), and depressants (e.g., alcohol or barbiturates) and their relationship to symptoms.

12. Conduct or refer the client for substance abuse evaluation/treatment. (See the Chemical Dependence chapter in this Planner.)

13. Refer the client to a physician for an evaluation as to

18. Obtain an adequate, stable sleep pattern. (7, 13, 35, 36)

19. Eat three nutritious meals per day. (5, 13, 37, 38, 39)

20. Increase the frequency of social contacts and the number of recreational activities that are involved in. (5, 13, 40, 41, 42)

21. Decrease psychomotor agitation. (13, 43)

22. Show evidence of daily care for personal grooming and hygiene with minimal reminders from others. (44, 45)

23. Use conflict resolution skills to state needs and resolve interpersonal issues that are contributing to depression. (46, 47)

24. Implement effective decision-making skills. (46, 48, 49)

25. Attend a support group for those with severe and persistent mental illness. (50)

26. Meet regularly with a volunteer mentor. (51)

27. Accept support from family members and a social support system. (52, 53, 54)

28. Agree to monitor symptoms and maintain ongoing treatment. (55, 56)

__. _____
   _____

__. _____
   _____

__. _____
   _____

the need for psychotropic medications.

14. Educate the client about the use and expected benefits of medication.

15. Monitor the client's medication compliance and effectiveness.

16. Review effects of the medications with the client and medical staff to identify possible side effects.

17. Monitor the client's other severe and persistent mental illness symptoms, which may be exacerbated by the introduction of an antidepressant.

18. Refer the client for individual and/or group psychotherapy with a therapist who specializes in the treatment of the severely and persistently mentally ill.

19. Ask the client to make a list of what he/she is depressed about and process this list with the clinician.

20. Encourage the client to identify and share the feelings of depression to clarify them and gain insight into the causes. Provide support and empathy.

21. Explore experiences from the client's past that may contribute to his/her depressed state.

22. Acknowledge the appropriateness of sadness or feelings of depression due to history of losses. (See the

Grief and Loss chapter in this Planner.)

23. Inquire about specific losses that severely and persistently mentally ill individuals experience (e.g., loss of independence, income, freedom, dignity or relationships) and how these losses may contribute to depression.

24. Provide the client with basic information about the causes and treatment of depression (e.g., see *The Depression Workbook* by Copeland).

25. Discuss the etiology of depression as it relates specifically to the client's symptoms and treatment.

26. Explain a connection between previously unexpressed (repressed) feelings, such as hurt, anger, or shame, and the current state of depression.

27. Assist the client in identifying specific emotions. Utilize a feelings poster, which graphically displays a variety of symptoms, if needed.

28. Teach or model healthy ways in which the client can express repressed emotions, including physical expressions (e.g., beating a pillow), verbal/written expressions (e.g., a letter), or rituals (e.g., writing the emotion down, then tearing it up and tossing into the wind).

29. Assess the client's ability to differentiate between severe and persistent mental illness symptoms (e.g., auditory hallucinations) and self-talk techniques.

30. Assign the client to keep a daily journal of experiences, automatic negative thoughts associated with experiences, and the depressive effect of distorted interpretation. Process this journal with clinician.

31. Teach the client positive, reality-based self-talk techniques (e.g., see *What to Say When You Talk to Yourself* by Helmstetter or *Ten Days to Self-Esteem* by Burns).

32. Reinforce positive, reality-based cognitive messages that enhance self-confidence and increase adaptive action.

33. Assist the client in identifying healthy, assertive ways to express anger.

34. Teach the client anger control techniques. (See the Anger Management chapter in this Planner.)

35. Review basic sleep hygiene needs (e.g., decrease stimulants in the evening; have a quiet, comfortable place to sleep; spend time winding down); reinforce structure to sleep routine.

36. Refer the client for a sleep disorder evaluation.

37. Urge the client to attempt to eat a small meal three times per day.

38. Facilitate the client in developing appropriate skills for selecting and preparing his/her own foods. (See the Activities of Daily Living chapter in this Planner.)

39. Refer the client to a dietician or nutritionist to evaluate needs for increasing appetite or food intake.

40. Refer the client to an activity therapist to identify social and recreational skills, and to develop a plan for exercise or social involvement. (See the Independent Activities of Daily Living or the Social Skills chapters in this Planner.)

41. Reinforce the client's participation in social activities and verbalization of feelings, needs, and desires.

42. Coordinate the client's involvement in volunteer opportunities with a social focus.

43. Teach the client deep muscle relaxation and deep breathing skills (e.g., see *The Depression Workbook* by Copeland).

44. Monitor and redirect the client on daily grooming and hygiene.

45. Teach the client personal hygiene skills. (See the Activities of Daily Living chapter in this Planner.)

46. Teach or refer the client for training in assertiveness skills (e.g., see *Asserting Yourself: A Practical Guide for Positive Change* by Brower).

47. Assist the client in developing solutions to relationship problems through facilitating a discussion with those from whom the client feels alienated; provide support and role playing of problem solving. (See the Intimate Relationship Conflicts or the Family Conflicts chapters in this Planner.)

48. Help the client to identify one decision that needs to be made. Break the decision down into smaller parts and focus the client on one portion at a time, examining the pros and cons of each choice.

49. Discourage the client from making major life decisions (when possible) until after his/her mood disorder improves.

50. Refer the client to a support group for individuals with chronic mental illness concerns.

51. Coordinate involvement with an individual/volunteer who will serve to mentor or befriend the client.

52. Educate the family about mental illness concerns with information (e.g., see *What to Do When Someone*

You Love Is Depressed: A Practical and Helpful Guide by Golant and Golant).

53. Provide feedback to the client and his/her family about the natural expression of negative emotions, differentiating between normal sadness and pathological depression symptoms.

54. Assist the client and his/her family in developing a family action plan, such as those described in *Troubled Journey* by Marsh and Dickens.

55. Educate the client about the ongoing need for maintenance treatment (e.g., keeping follow-up case manager and physician appointments, taking medication consistently, attending support groups, etc.) despite the lack of identifiable symptoms.

56. Request the client to identify a list of symptom triggers and indicators. Urge the client to share this information with a support network to assist in monitoring the symptoms.

__. _____

_____

__. _____

_____

__. _____

_____

DIAGNOSTIC SUGGESTIONS

Axis I:	297.1	Delusional Disorder
	295.xx	Schizophrenia
	295.10	Schizophrenia, Disorganized Type
	295.30	Schizophrenia, Paranoid Type
	295.70	Schizoaffective Disorder
	296.xx	Bipolar I Disorder
	296.89	Bipolar II Disorder
	296.2x	Major Depressive Disorder, Single Episode
	296.3x	Major Depressive Disorder, Recurrent
	309.0	Adjustment Disorder With Depressed Mood
	V62.82	Bereavement
	V62.89	Phase-of-Life Problem
	_____	_____
	_____	_____

EMPLOYMENT PROBLEMS

BEHAVIORAL DEFINITIONS

1. Chronic periods of unemployment or underemployment.
2. History of multiple occupational terminations due to interpersonal conflict or inability to control primary psychosis symptoms (i.e., manic phases, hallucinations, or delusions).
3. Decreased desire to actively seek employment or maintain current position.
4. Lack of formal training or on-the-job experience.
5. Failure to achieve or maintain expected levels of occupational involvement, duration, and success.
6. Rebellion against and/or conflicts with authority figures due to unfounded suspiciousness or paranoia.
7. Feelings of anxiety, depression, or other psychiatric destabilization secondary to being fired or laid off.
8. Verbalized fears about returning to the workplace due to a history of employment problems and failures.
9. Feelings of anxiety or depression that are related to the menial or repetitive nature of job placement.
10. Exacerbation of primary psychosis symptoms due to the anxiety of new employment or increased job tasks/expectations.

__. _____
   _____
   _____
__. _____
   _____
   _____
__. _____
   _____

LONG-TERM GOALS

1. Develop positive skills for getting along in the work environment.
2. Obtain occupational skills that are necessary to gain entry-level or advanced positions.
3. Control primary psychosis symptoms to manageable levels while in the workplace.
4. Increase desire to be actively involved in obtaining and maintaining employment.
5. Identify and coordinate basic supports that are needed to obtain and maintain employment.
6. Understand how chronic mental illness symptoms impact on employment opportunities.
7. Learn skills for identifying and resolving problems with coworkers and supervisor.
8. Express fears and disappointment that are relative to employment history and satisfaction.

—. _____
   _____
   _____
—. _____
   _____
   _____
—. _____
   _____

SHORT-TERM OBJECTIVES	THERAPEUTIC INTERVENTIONS
1. Share the history of employment. (1, 2)	1. Assist the client in preparing a chronological outline of previous employment.
2. Identify positive and negative experiences in employment. (3, 4)	2. Review employment history with the client to identify patterns of success and failure.
3. Identify the role of mental illness symptoms in employment difficulties. (4, 5, 6)	3. Ask the client to describe two previous successful employment situations.
4. Attend appointments consistently with a physician for psychotropic medication evaluation. (7)	4. Ask the client to describe two negative job experiences, listening attentively

5. Take antipsychotic medications consistently as prescribed. (8, 9)

6. Report the side effects and effectiveness of medications to an appropriate professional. (10, 11)

7. Verbalize an understanding of the positive effects of medications on employment skills and functioning. (12)

8. Identify three interpersonal behaviors that will promote success and understanding in the workplace. (13)

9. Implement prosocial behavior changes in the employment environment. (14, 15)

10. Utilize assertiveness to communicate basic needs to the employer. (16, 17)

11. Identify the reasons for not obtaining or maintaining employment. (18, 19)

12. List positive reasons to seek and maintain employment. (20)

13. Identify skills for possible job placement. (1, 21, 22, 23, 24)

14. Remediate basic occupational deficits. (24, 25)

15. Express a desire for one or more specific job placements. (26, 27)

16. Develop a resume. (28)

17. Obtain letter(s) of reference. (29)

18. Utilize classified advertisements for a job search. (30, 31)

to the circumstances and emotions.

5. Request that the client identify two situations in which the primary symptoms of his/her mental illness have negatively affected his/her job performance or social interaction at work.

6. Educate the client about the expected or common symptoms of his/her mental illness, which impact upon his/her employment (i.e., mania, paranoia, or negative symptoms of schizophrenia).

7. Arrange for a psychiatric evaluation to assess the need for antipsychotic or other psychiatric medications, and arrange a prescription, if appropriate.

8. Encourage the client to take his/her medications consistently.

9. Coordinate the availability of a secure, private area where the client can keep and take medications while at the work site, if necessary.

10. Monitor the client for medication compliance, effectiveness, and side effects, referring back to physician as necessary for medication evaluation/adjustment.

11. Educate the client about the use of and the expected benefits of psychiatric medications.

19. Demonstrate job interview skills. (32, 33)

20. Successfully complete an interview and obtain a job offer. (34, 35, 36)

21. Cooperate with a job coach to improve performance skills on the job. (37)

22. Agree to share information regarding mental illness with people at the work setting. (38, 39)

23. Dress and groom appropriately and follow the rules of the workplace. (40, 41, 42)

—. _____
_____

—. _____
_____

—. _____
_____

12. Educate the client about the expected positive effect on common psychiatric symptoms of his/her mental illness, which impact upon employment functioning (i.e., paranoia, mania).

13. Assist the client in identifying three social behaviors (i.e., eye contact, dress, and politeness) on which to focus, which will promote better interpersonal functioning in a work situation.

14. Assist the client in identifying situations in which new prosocial behaviors have been or could be utilized.

15. Use behavioral rehearsal, role playing, and role reversal to practice targeted interpersonal behavior; urge implementation in vivo.

16. Teach assertiveness skills, utilizing principals in *The Assertiveness Workbook* by Pfeiffer or *Assert Yourself* by Lindenfield.

17. Refer the client to an assertiveness training workshop, which will educate the client and facilitate assertiveness skills via lectures, assignments, and role playing.

18. Assist the client in identifying possible reasons for not obtaining employment (e.g., loss of disability payments, fear of increased responsibility or expectations).

19. Assist the client in evaluating or processing reasons

for not obtaining or maintaining employment.

20. Assist the client with identifying positive reasons for
obtaining or maintaining
employment.

21. Help the client identify
marketable skills for which
he/she has displayed mas-
tery.

22. Refer the client for a psychological evaluation to
identify cognitive abilities
and deficits.

23. Administer or arrange for
aptitude testing to identify
specific job skills.

24. Refer the client to a skill assessment and training program (e.g., community
education, technical center,
vocational rehabilitation, or
occupational therapy).

25. Monitor the client's ongoing
attendance, functioning in,
and progress in educational
or rehabilitation programming.

26. Utilize interest testing
such as the Strong Voca-
tional Interest Blank to
identify specific types of oc-
cupations in which the
client has interest.

27. Review interest testing
with the client to brain-
storm occupational place-
ments.

28. Assist the client in develop-
ing a resume using *101
Quick Tips for a Dynamite
Resume* by Fein or *Resumes*

for the First Time Job Hunter by the VGM Career Horizons editors.

29. Request that the client identify family, friends, teachers, former employers, or other clinicians from whom letters of reference may be requested; assign the procurement of these letters.

30. Review local want ads with the client.

31. Request that the client identify two or three jobs from the classified ads for which he/she would like to apply.

32. Assign the client to read selections from *What Color Is Your Parachute?* by Bowles or *10 Minute Guide to Job Interviews* by Morgan.

33. Utilize role playing behavioral rehearsal and role reversal to increase the client's confidence and skill in the interview process.

34. Assist the client in planning an interview appointment.

35. Coordinate the client's transportation to the interview if needed.

36. Process the interview and assist with the decision-making process about accepting the job offer.

37. Arrange for a job coach to meet regularly with the client in the job setting to review job needs, skills, and problem areas.

38. With the proper release, review the client's mental illness symptoms with the employer.

39. With the proper release, provide information about mental illness concerns and sensitivity training to the client's fellow employees.

40. Visit the client at the job site often, giving him/her feedback about hygiene, dress, behavior, and technical skills.

41. Review the workplace rules and etiquette regularly.

42. Meet with the employer regularly to review the client's functioning and needs, tapering over time.

__. _____

_____

__. _____

_____

__. _____

_____

DIAGNOSTIC SUGGESTIONS

Axis I:	297.1	Delusional Disorder
	295.xx	Schizophrenia
	295.10	Schizophrenia, Disorganized Type
	295.30	Schizophrenia, Paranoid Type
	295.70	Schizoaffective Disorder
	296.xx	Bipolar I Disorder
	296.89	Bipolar II Disorder
	V62.2	Occupational Problem
	V62.89	Phase-of-Life Problem
	_____	_____
	_____	_____

FAMILY CONFLICTS

BEHAVIORAL DEFINITIONS

1. Estranged relationships with family members.
2. Abusive, manipulative, or intimidating behavior toward family members.
3. Lower-than-expected functioning in a variety of areas due to over-control of the client's basic needs and decisions by the family.
4. Family members' failure to accept the mentally ill individual, or his/her diagnosis of a mental illness.
5. Limited knowledge of chronic mental illness symptoms and indicators of decompensation by family members.
6. Lack of understanding of treatment options by family members.
7. Family members are embarrassed and hide the client because of his/her erratic behaviors related to psychosis or other severe mental illness.

—. _____

_____

—. _____

_____

—. _____

_____

LONG-TERM GOALS

1. Rebuild important family relationships.
2. Experience acceptance from family members.
3. Make personal decisions with minimal or least restrictive oversight.

4. Behave in a direct, assertive, and loving way toward family members.
5. Family members learn about mental illness symptoms, prodromals, possible causes, and expected duration of illness.
6. Family members gain an understanding of and an involvement in the treatment options that are available to the client.
7. Advocacy in the community by family members.

—. _____
_____
_____

—. _____
_____
_____

—. _____
_____

SHORT-TERM OBJECTIVES

1. Describe the history of family relationships. (1, 2, 3)
2. Identify problematic relationships in the family system. (2, 3, 4)
3. Describe healthy and positive relationships in the family system. (2, 3, 5, 6, 7)
4. Family members express and clarify their feelings about the client's mental illness and its impact on the family. (8)
5. Family members identify the impact of the client's mental illness symptoms on the family system. (9)
6. Family members read literature about mental illness symptoms. (10, 11)
7. Family members attend support groups for the family of the mentally ill. (12, 13)

THERAPEUTIC INTERVENTIONS

1. Request that the client identify and describe family relationships.
2. Request that the client provide two examples of positive and two examples of negative family experiences.
3. Develop a genogram based on the client's description of the family.
4. Request that the client list and describe problematic relationships. Process with a clinician.
5. Request that the client list and describe positive relationships.
6. Clarify any patterns to the client's behavior that contribute to positive and negative relationships and interactions.

8. Family members ask questions freely about mental illness to increase understanding and eradicate myths. (12, 14)

9. Family members verbalize an understanding of the client's specific behaviors and symptoms. (15, 16, 17, 18)

10. Family members verbalize an understanding of the treatment options that are available to the client. (15, 19, 20)

11. Family members increase their involvement in the client's treatment. (21, 22, 23)

12. Obtain assistance from the family in monitoring the regular use of prescribed medications. (24, 25)

13. Exchange thoughts and feelings with the family members regarding the client's mental illness symptoms. (8, 26, 27, 28)

14. Experience acceptance from the client's family despite his/her mental illness symptoms. (5, 28, 29, 30)

15. List enjoyable leisure activities to which the family can be invited, or in which their participation would be desired. (31, 32)

16. Reestablish estranged family relationships. (4, 28, 31, 33)

7. Utilize solution-focused techniques to help the client identify how he/she has facilitated positive interactions in the past.

8. Facilitate the family members in identifying and expressing emotions to a clinician regarding the client's mental illness.

9. Use the magical question (i.e., "What would happen in your family if the client did not have any mental illness symptoms?") to help the family identify the impact of the mental illness symptoms on the family.

10. Assign readings from *Surviving Schizophrenia* by Torrey, *Depression: How it Happens, How It's Healed* by Medina, or similar sources to help family members better understand severe mental illness.

11. Refer the client and his/her family to a lending library at the agency or in the community to access books or tapes on severe mental illness.

12. Refer the parents to or conduct didactic sessions on the topic of psychosis.

13. Refer the parents to a support group for families of the mentally ill.

14. Identify yourself and other clinicians as available to answer family questions about mental illness.

17. Family members reduce the frequency of speaking for the client or performing activities that the client is capable of doing independently. (12, 13, 34, 35, 36)

18. Make all decisions to the maximum of the client's capability to increase independent functioning. (36, 37)

19. Decrease incidents of aggressive acting out toward the family. (38, 39, 40)

20. Family to network with others who are facing similar problem areas. (13, 22, 41)

21. Family to identify and engage in a support network that can reduce the stress of caring for a mentally ill family member. (42, 43, 44)

22. Family to schedule and attend appointments with professionals who can assist them with financial or spiritual needs. (45)

23. Obtain needed day-to-day assistance from family members rather than from treatment staff. (46, 47)

24. Family to identify a plan for dealing with a crisis in the client's behavior due to decompensation. (48)

25. Family to develop long-term plans for care and advocacy of the client relative to aging parents or the potential loss of the primary advocate/caregiver. (13, 22, 23, 49, 50)

15. Obtain a written release of information from the client allowing the clinician to provide specific information about the client's mental illness symptoms and treatment to the family.

16. Meet regularly with family members to discuss the client's history of mental illness symptoms and treatment.

17. Encourage family members to hold each other accountable for healthy responses to the client's behavior and symptoms.

18. Help the family to see the client's symptoms as part of an illness rather than as laziness or hostility.

19. Assign reading from *Schizophrenia: The Facts* by Tsuang and Faraone, *The Depression Sourcebook* by Quinn, *Helping Someone With Mental Illness* by Carter and Golant, or similar sources to assist the family in understanding treatment options for severe mental illness.

20. Review the client's specific treatment interventions with family members, focusing on answering their questions and concerns.

21. Encourage family members to attend treatment planning sessions.

22. Provide opportunities for family members to be in-

26. Maintain involvement in family spiritual practices. (51, 52, 53)

27. Family members to verbalize resolution of feelings of guilt and responsibility for the client's mental illness. (54)

__. _____
   _____
__. _____
   _____
__. _____
   _____

volved in advocacy groups and agency committees.

23. Assign a separate clinician to act as a family advocate who will provide information regarding mental illness signs and treatment, feedback regarding the client's progress, and advocacy to the family.

24. Encourage the client, family, and prescribing physician to exchange information regarding symptoms, medications, and side effects.

25. Request that the family assist in monitoring the client's medication use and compliance.

26. Teach assertiveness skills to the client and his/her family to assist in the expression of emotions.

27. Provide empathetic listening to the client and his/her family as they express emotional content to help them clarify their feelings.

28. Coordinate ongoing family therapy sessions to assist the client and his/her family in expressing their emotions and needs and in finding solutions to conflicts.

29. Encourage the family members to express acceptance of the client directly, or through a letter of acceptance.

30. Facilitate the client in expressing appreciation for

assistance and acceptance from family members.

31. Assist the client in identifying mutually satisfying social activities for himself/herself and his/her family.

32. Refer to an activity or a recreational therapist for assistance in developing leisure skills to share with family members.

33. Coordinate contact with estranged family members.

34. Identify roles in the family and behavioral patterns that developed in the family's reaction to mental illness symptoms that have inappropriately limited the client's independent functioning and enabled dependence.

35. Monitor the client's progress at specified intervals and report this information to the client and his/her family.

36. Provide the family with the training that is needed to support the client's advancement, including training in person-centered planning processes (e.g., mental illness signs and symptoms, and advocacy).

37. Encourage the client (and encourage the family to allow the client) to make all possible choices and demonstrate maximum independence in daily events.

38. Monitor the client's pro-dromals.

39. Provide the family with information regarding the client's prodromals relative to aggressive decompensation.

40. Provide the client with training and opportunities to express anger and other emotions in healthy ways (e.g., journaling, beating on a pillow, assertiveness).

41. Coordinate a mentoring or matching program for stable and struggling families to assist each other.

42. Assess the family's support network (e.g., extended family, neighbors, church friends, social relationships, etc.) that provides diversion, emotional support, and/or respite care for the client.

43. Refer the family to community-based respite services, coordinating for others to provide supervision or to take responsibility for the client on a short-term basis.

44. Acknowledge the family's frustration and anger regarding not having received services that they desired in the past, attempting now to redirect them to available services.

45. Refer the family to ancillary services such as financial counseling or spiritual counseling.

46. Educate the family members on assertiveness skills, techniques for managing the client's symptoms, and problem solving.

47. Link the client and his/her family members to a variety of formal resources and informal supports.

48. Develop and review consistently the family's plan for how to deal with a crisis in the client's behavior, thinking, or mood, and when to utilize a crisis line for assistance.

49. Review the options that will be available should the primary caregiver/advocate be unable to care for the client.

50. Encourage the ongoing involvement of non–mentally ill siblings in treatment and social contact with the client.

51. Encourage the family members to continue normal involvement of the client in church or other religious behaviors if they are a part of the family's spiritual practice.

52. Monitor mental illness symptoms related to religious themes, and provide feedback to the client about such.

53. With the proper release of information, give the information to the clergy or other church leaders regarding assistance that the

client may need in accessing spiritual practices and
programs.

54. Assist the family members
in resolving any unrealistic
feelings of responsibility
and self-blame for the
client's mental illness.

___. _____
_____
___. _____
_____
___. _____
_____

DIAGNOSTIC SUGGESTIONS

Axis I:	297.1	Delusional Disorder
	295.xx	Schizophrenia
	295.10	Schizophrenia, Disorganized Type
	295.30	Schizophrenia, Paranoid Type
	295.90	Schizophrenia, Undifferentiated Type
	295.60	Schizophrenia, Residual Type
	295.70	Schizoaffective Disorder
	296.xx	Bipolar I Disorder
	296.89	Bipolar II Disorder
	V61.20	Parent-Child Relational Problem
	V61.1	Partner Relational Problem
	V61.8	Sibling Relational Problem
	_____	_____
	_____	_____

FINANCIAL NEEDS

BEHAVIORAL DEFINITIONS

1. Low income due to the effects of psychotic and other severe mental illness symptoms.
2. Chronic homelessness or constant use of supported transitional living services, such as homeless shelters or adult foster care placements.
3. Lack of consistent, adequate employment that is capable of providing funds for basic needs.
4. Impulsive or excessive spending due to psychotic or manic episodes.
5. Failure to plan, organize, or budget for basic financial responsibilities.
6. History of not applying for or accessing monetary entitlements or other available welfare benefits.
7. Engagement in illegal activity to meet financial needs.
8. Poor credit history, or an inability to qualify for credit.

__. _____
   _____
   _____
__. _____
   _____
   _____
__. _____
   _____

LONG-TERM GOALS

1. Establish a stable, permanent, legal income that meets basic financial needs.

2. Find living arrangements that are either government supported, independent, or provided by family, and that are stable, safe, and secure.
3. Find full- or part-time employment at a position that is well suited to the client's abilities and with employer/coworkers who are tolerant of the client's mental illness symptoms.
4. Generate a realistic plan for short-term, as well as long-term, financial stability.
5. Display budgeting skills as evidenced by adherence to a written budget and paying bills on a timely basis.
6. Utilize or apply for appropriate, available, and necessary entitlements or other benefits.

—. _____
   _____
   _____
—. _____
   _____
   _____
—. _____
   _____

SHORT-TERM OBJECTIVES

1. Describe the history of financial issues and the details of current financial situation. (1, 2)
2. Identify both positive and negative financial practices. (2, 3, 4, 5)
3. List current financial needs and obligations. (6, 7)
4. Identify how mental illness symptoms affect financial concerns. (8, 9)
5. Decrease immediate access to funds to limit erratic, impulsive spending. (10, 11, 12, 13)
6. Use medication to decrease the mental illness symp-

THERAPEUTIC INTERVENTIONS

1. Request that the client relate his/her history or pattern of financial concerns.
2. Provide the client with support and empathy, focusing on decreasing his/her guilt or blame for financial difficulties.
3. Request that the client identify at least two financial practices that he/she uses that are beneficial or that add to stability (e.g., saving, budgeting, comparison shopping).
4. Assist the client in identifying at least two financial practices that have led to

toms that might affect financial abilities or lead to impulsive, erratic spending. (14, 15, 16)

7. Establish a stable residence that is not dependent on personal finance management. (17, 18)

8. Obtain a more independent residence, and maintain responsible control over finances. (19, 20)

9. Obtain all necessary public welfare benefits to provide funds for general use. (21, 22, 23, 24)

10. Secure ancillary public and private benefits or grants for specific financial needs (i.e., heating bills, education, etc.). (25, 26)

11. Obtain public or private insurance to assist with payment for medical and psychiatric services. (27)

12. Write a basic budget that will control spending. (6, 28, 29, 30)

13. Develop a long-term financial plan. (31)

14. Practice basic banking techniques. (32, 33, 34, 35)

—. _____
_____

—. _____
_____

—. _____
_____

difficulty (e.g., unstable work history, impulsive spending, failure to pay on commitments).

5. Process financial successes and failures, focusing on patterns, triggers, and consequences of successes and failures.

6. Direct the client to write out a list of all current financial obligations.

7. Compare the client's list of financial obligations with normally expected obligations (e.g., see those listed on the budgeting worksheet in _Personal Budget Planner: A Guide for Financial Success_ by Gelb); process any discrepancies from normal expectations.

8. Educate the client about the typical symptoms that are expected in his/her mental illness.

9. Assist the client in identifying at least two ways in which his/her mental illness has affected financial concerns.

10. Suggest to the client that he/she voluntarily allow someone else to be his/her payee, or otherwise exercise general control over his/her finances.

11. Assist the client in initiating legal procedures for obtaining a payee for benefits.

12. Coordinate for a cosigner to be necessary for all bank withdrawal transactions.

13. Pursue involuntary legal control over the client's finances through guardianship processes.

14. Arrange for a psychiatric evaluation and coordinate medications, if necessary.

15. Educate the client about the use of and expected benefit from medications.

16. Monitor the client's medication compliance, effectiveness, and side effects.

17. Coordinate for an adult foster care placement if the client is unable to manage finances even with assistance.

18. Coordinate an arrangement for the client to live with family members or friends.

19. Assist the client in developing an independent or semi-independent living situation with necessary supports related to financial and other areas.

20. Meet regularly to review the client's financial needs and money management practices.

21. Assist the client in obtaining, completing, and filing forms for Social Security Disability benefits or other public aid.

22. Coordinate transportation for the client to necessary appointments related to obtaining benefits.

23. Refer the client to specific readings in *How to Get Every Penny You're Entitled*

to *From Social Security* by Bosley and Gurwitz.

24. Provide an agency address as a possible mail drop to which a homeless client may have his/her government benefit check sent.

25. Compile and provide to the client a list of available and relevant financial assistance resources in his/her area (i.e., home heating assistance, scholarships, housing funds).

26. Assist the client with scheduling, filling out forms, and obtaining transportation to obtain assistance from area programs, as necessary.

27. Coordinate the client's application for Medicaid, Medicare, or other applicable public or private insurance.

28. Educate the client in basic budgeting skills (e.g., see *Personal Budget Planner: A Guide for Financial Success* by Gelb).

29. Request that the client develop a basic budget, including income, basic expenses, additional spending, and savings plans.

30. Refer the client to a community education class related to basic finances.

31. Request that the client identify realistic, long-term financial plans. Process with a clinician.

32. Educate the client about typical banking procedures.

33. Assist the client in obtaining proper identification (i.e., a state identification card) necessary for banking functions.

34. Coordinate for the client to receive a hands-on tour of a bank, with a focus on him/her becoming more comfortable with the procedures and security measures.

35. Practice banking procedures such as check writing and cashing, using imitation supplies or forms.

__. _____
_____
__. _____
_____
__. _____
_____

DIAGNOSTIC SUGGESTIONS

Axis I:	297.1	Delusional Disorder
	295.xx	Schizophrenia
	295.10	Schizophrenia, Disorganized Type
	295.30	Schizophrenia, Paranoid Type
	295.90	Schizophrenia, Undifferentiated Type
	295.60	Schizophrenia, Residual Type
	295.70	Schizoaffective Disorder
	296.xx	Bipolar I Disorder
	296.89	Bipolar II Disorder
	V62.2	Occupational Problem
	V62.89	Phase-of-Life Problem
	____	_____
	____	_____

GRIEF AND LOSS

BEHAVIORAL DEFINITIONS

1. Death of a significant other resulting in depression, confusion, and feelings of insecurity regarding the future.
2. Thoughts that are dominated by the loss, culminating in confusion, disorganized behavior, and exacerbation of mental illness symptoms.
3. Exhibits signs and symptoms of depression, including changes in eating or sleeping patterns, thoughts of suicide, crying, or depressed mood.
4. Feelings of hopelessness, worthlessness, inappropriate guilt, or a fear of abandonment due to multiple losses.
5. Avoidance of situations, conversations, or thoughts that recall the losses.
6. Loss of abilities, status, or competence due to incapacitating effects of psychotic and other severe mental illness symptoms.
7. Feelings of low self-esteem that are associated with a history of losses.
8. Description of childhood traumas, sexual assault, or abusive parent figures.
9. Dissociative phenomena or exacerbations of paranoia.
10. Ongoing (nondelusional) spiritual conflicts.
11. Loss of support network due to effects of psychotic and other severe mental illness symptoms.

—. _____
   _____
   _____
—. _____
   _____
—. _____
   _____

LONG-TERM GOALS

1. Accept the loss and return to stable level of functioning.
2. Express unresolved emotions regarding losses.
3. Display an understanding of the grief process and how this process may be exacerbated by or may exacerbate mental illness symptoms.
4. Develop an understanding of how avoidance of the grief process may affect functioning in many areas.
5. Understand the relationship between mental illness symptoms and losses.
6. Identify realistic goals and plans that are relative to losses and mental illness symptoms.
7. Develop alternative diversions and other coping mechanisms that are related to loss issues.
8. Decrease negative emotions that are directly related to the failure to grieve losses.
9. Resolve spiritual conflict.
10. Redevelop a supportive social system.

—. _____
   _____
—. _____
   _____
—. _____
   _____

SHORT-TERM OBJECTIVES

1. Describe the loss of significant others. (1)
2. Identify crisis grief and loss symptoms. (1, 2, 3)
3. Identify losses due to relationship difficulties. (3, 4, 5)
4. Identify losses of occupational and other functional abilities. (3, 6, 7)
5. Express feelings regarding the experience of the loss. (8)

THERAPEUTIC INTERVENTIONS

1. Provide the client with direct emotional support through active and empathic listening regarding grief issues.
2. Assess the client for suicidal intent.
3. Refer the suicidal client to a psychiatric hospital or crisis residential placement to pro-

6. Take psychotropic medications as prescribed. (9, 10, 11)

7. Report the side effects and effectiveness of medications to the appropriate professional. (10, 11, 12)

8. Verbalize an understanding of the basic grief process. (13, 14)

9. Express an understanding of mental illness symptoms that are related to own diagnosis. (15, 16, 17)

10. Identify defense mechanisms (e.g., denial, minimalization, or rationalization) that are related to the avoidance of grief. (18, 19)

11. Identify how mental illness symptoms have contributed to losses in life. (4, 6, 20, 21)

12. Identify and express basic emotions. (22, 23, 24)

13. Journal emotions that are related to the losses. (1, 8, 25, 26)

14. Verbalize acceptance of losses without being overwhelmed with grief, anger, or fear. (27, 28)

15. Implement rituals that begin to bring a feeling of closure to the emotions that are related to the losses. (29, 30, 31)

16. Generate alternative diversions to losses. (31, 32)

17. Express spiritual concerns that are related to losses. (33, 34)

vide him/her 24-hour-per-day monitoring and safety.

4. Request that the client prepare a list of important relationships that have been lost; process factors contributing to the loss.

5. Assist the client in resolving relationship problems. (See the Social Skills chapter in this Planner.)

6. Request that the client prepare a list of job losses and other related losses due to mental illness symptoms.

7. Assist the client in resolving relationship problems. (See the Employment Problems chapter in this Planner.)

8. Provide the client with an opportunity to vent emotions that are related to losses, symptoms, or setbacks.

9. Refer the client to a physician for a psychiatric evaluation to assess the need for antidepressant or other psychotropic medication.

10. Educate the client about the use, expected benefits, and possible side effects of medications.

11. Monitor the client's compliance with prescription medication, its side effects, and its effectiveness.

12. Urge and reinforce a strict compliance with the medication prescription, assessing for refusal or abuse of medication.

18. Obtain support from loved ones or others who are experiencing similar problems. (17, 35)

—. _____
   _____

—. _____
   _____

—. _____
   _____

13. Assign readings from *The Grief Recovery Handbook: The Action Program for Moving Beyond Death* by James and Friedman to assist in understanding typical grief patterns.

14. Teach the client regarding the grief process and help him/her to understand the stage of the grief process in which he/she is currently.

15. Educate the client about the mental illness symptoms that are related to his/her diagnosis.

16. Review the client's mental illness symptoms, focusing on the impact that these have had on his/her losses.

17. Refer the client to a support group for individuals with mental illness problems.

18. Educate the client about the use of defense mechanisms and provide specific examples (e.g., some individuals deny problems rather than face the reality of a chronic mental illness).

19. Assist the client in identifying ways in which he/she uses defense mechanisms to delay or avoid grief and loss issues.

20. Assign and process readings from *Grieving Mental Illness: A Guide for Patients and Their Caregivers* by Lafond.

21. Request that the client develop a list of ways in which

the mental illness symptoms have affected him/her; process with a clinician.

22. Review a list of basic emotions and discuss the social, verbal, and body language cues that help to identify them.

23. Ask the client to list ways in which he/she identifies and labels specific emotions that are experienced.

24. Help the client learn to identify emotions by probing for clarification of his/her unidentified emotional states.

25. Request that the client write in a journal or record on an audiotape the feelings of grief that he/she experienced with relation to the losses, and then share these with a clinician.

26. Process the client's identified grief issues.

27. Request that the client write in a journal or record on an audiotape his/her feelings of acceptance of the losses, and share these with a clinician.

28. Assign and process readings from *Forgive and Forget: Healing the Hurts We Don't Deserve* by Smedes to help the client overcome resentment.

29. Encourage and coordinate the client's utilization of typical mourning events (e.g., visit the gravesite of a deceased relative, write a

good-bye letter to someone who is deceased, etc.).

30. Assist the client in developing and safely carrying out meaningful rituals for letting go of a loss (i.e., tying a journal entry, letter, or picture to a helium balloon and letting it go).

31. Assist the client in developing meaningful activities that assist in resolving grief issues (e.g., volunteer to help in a support group that focuses on his/her loss issue).

32. Encourage and coordinate the client's increased involvement in social activities, hobbies, or volunteer placements.

33. Suggest that the client read *How Can It Be All Right When Everything Is All Wrong?* by Smedes, *When Bad Things Happen to Good People* by Kushner, or other readings that are suitable to his/her faith.

34. Explore the client's spiritual struggles and, if necessary, refer him/her to an appropriate clergy person to allow for further discussion of these issues.

35. Coordinate a family therapy session that is focused on the client's history of losses to enhance family members' understanding and support of the client.

—. _____
    _____
—. _____
    _____
—. _____
    _____

DIAGNOSTIC SUGGESTIONS

Axis I:

297.1	Delusional Disorder
295.xx	Schizophrenia
295.10	Schizophrenia, Disorganized Type
295.30	Schizophrenia, Paranoid Type
295.70	Schizoaffective Disorder
296.xx	Bipolar I Disorder
296.89	Bipolar II Disorder
296.3x	Major Depressive Disorder, Recurrent
309.xx	Adjustment Disorder, Chronic
V62.82	Bereavement
V62.89	Phase-of-Life Problem
_____	_____
_____	_____

HEALTH ISSUES

BEHAVIORAL DEFINITIONS

1. A diagnosed, serious medical condition that needs attention and that has an impact on daily living (e.g., high blood pressure, asthma, seizures, diabetes, heart disease, cancer, or cirrhosis).
2. Under a physician's care for a medical condition.
3. A positive test for human immunodeficiency virus (HIV) or acquired immune deficiency syndrome (AIDS).
4. Limited understanding of medical needs, treatment options, and available medical services.
5. Difficulties with gaining access to medical facilities or health care providers.
6. Failure to access medical treatment due to psychotic or other severe and persistent mental illness symptoms.
7. Poor health habits including poor oral hygiene, infrequent bathing, or unsanitary living conditions.
8. Failure to access or follow through with medical treatment due to financial limitations.
9. Medical complications secondary to substance abuse.

__. _____

_____

__. _____

_____

__. _____

_____

LONG-TERM GOALS

1. Stabilize medical condition.
2. Accept the reality of current medical problems.
3. Develop and implement an active, comprehensive plan for treatment of medical problem(s).
4. Take responsibility for physical health and well-being.
5. Establish a trusting relationship with a physician who is knowledgeable about working with mentally ill patients.
6. Maintain good personal hygiene.
7. Obtain health insurance coverage.
8. Access health care through public assistance.

—. _____
   _____

—. _____
   _____

—. _____
   _____

SHORT-TERM OBJECTIVES

1. Determine current medical problems. (1, 2)
2. Stabilize the crisis with medical problems. (3, 4, 5)
3. Verbalize and accept the reality of the current medical difficulties. (4, 6, 7)
4. Family, friends, and support network learn about medical problems and needs. (8, 9)
5. Implement a stable, healthy, and appealing diet. (4, 10, 11, 12)
6. Follow through with a referral to a dietician. (13)
7. Terminate the abuse of mood-altering substances. (14, 15, 16)

THERAPEUTIC INTERVENTIONS

1. Arrange for an immediate physical examination to determine physical health needs.
2. Coordinate the necessary medical testing.
3. Consult with a physician about the needed medical treatment.
4. Educate the client about his/her current medical problems and the treatment options. Assist the client in decisions about his/her current medical treatment needs.

8. Implement good personal hygiene behaviors. (17, 18, 19)

9. Follow an exercise plan. (20, 21, 22, 23)

10. Maintain personal health through regular checkups. (24, 25, 26, 27, 28)

11. Maintain good oral hygiene. (29, 30)

12. Preserve or remediate hearing and vision capabilities. (31)

13. Obtain the needed resources for payment for ongoing health care. (32, 33, 34)

14. Decrease medical difficulties related to transience or homelessness by maintaining a stable residence. (35, 36, 37)

15. Take psychotropic medications as prescribed. (38, 39, 40, 41)

16. Report regarding the side effects and the effectiveness of medications. (40, 41, 42, 43)

17. Decrease the likelihood of HIV infection or other sexually transmitted diseases (STDs) by implementing safer sex practices. (44, 45, 46, 47, 48)

18. Decrease violence or abuse by partners. (36, 48, 49, 50)

19. Caretakers verbalize the degree of emotional strain that is related to providing care to the client with a co-

5. Assist the client in making arrangements for the necessary medical treatment.

6. Assist the client in acknowledging an emotional desire to deny or avoid the truth about his/her medical difficulties.

7. Reinforce the client's acceptance of the reality of his/her medical problems.

8. Obtain a proper release of information to provide family, friends, and others with information regarding the client's medical needs.

9. Encourage family, friends, and the support network to provide emotional support and positive reinforcement for the client's adherence to medical treatment.

10. Educate the client about healthy food choices and the effect of diet on long-term medical well-being.

11. Assist the client with access to a grocery store, focusing on increasing his/her comfort level.

12. Educate the client about food shopping choices and how to compare healthy foods with unhealthy.

13. Refer to a dietician for an assessment of dietary needs, strengths, and weaknesses.

14. Assess or refer the client to a substance abuse evaluator to determine the presence of

morbid health concern.
(8, 51, 52)

20. Caretakers report reduced stress that is related to providing care to the client with a comorbid health concern. (52, 53, 54)

__. _____

   _____

__. _____

   _____

__. _____

   _____

a concomitant substance abuse problem.

15. Refer the client for substance abuse treatment. (See the Chemical Dependence chapter in this Planner.)

16. Educate the client about the short- and long-term effects of substance abuse.

17. Assess the client's personal hygiene needs. Encourage him/her to discuss his/her views of his/her own needs. (See the IADL chapter in this Planner.)

18. Refer the client to a training group for basic hygiene needs.

19. Institute a checklist and reinforcement system for the client regarding hygiene needs.

20. Teach the client about the regular use of exercise and the health benefits that are related to exercise.

21. Refer the client to an activity therapist to assist in the development of an enjoyable, practical exercise program.

22. Refer the client to an agency- or community-sponsored exercise group.

23. Coordinate the client obtaining a free or reduced-cost membership to a local health club.

24. Coordinate a referral to a general physician for routine and ongoing medical evaluation and care.

25. Schedule an intermittent, planned psychiatric hospitalization to complete all needed medical services in a structured, safe, familiar setting.

26. Facilitate transportation to medical, dental, and other health care appointments. Monitor the client's attendance to these appointments.

27. Obtain a release of information to share information with other health care providers. Educate the providers about the client's needs relative to mental illness symptoms.

28. Broker appointments with a doctor's office (i.e., request that the scheduling receptionist contact a clinician regarding appointment changes, etc., so the clinician can guarantee the client's attendance).

29. Coordinate biannual dental checkups and cleanings.

30. Train and encourage regular brushing and flossing. Reinforce with positive feedback.

31. Coordinate hearing and vision evaluations. Assist the client in following up on recommendations.

32. Coordinate health care services through an agency staff when it's possible and appropriate.

33. Assist the client in filing for and maintaining public assistance, benefits, and insurance.

34. Refer the client to an agency list of health care providers who accept public insurance or provide services at a reduced cost or at no cost.

35. Assist the client in developing or maintaining his/her stable residence. (See the Homelessness chapter in this Planner.)

36. Refer the client to a personal safety class (e.g., self-defense, precautions for safety).

37. Deliver health care services to the client where he/she is accessible (i.e., in a homeless shelter or on the street through mobile health vans).

38. Arrange for a psychiatric evaluation with a physician who is informed and knowledgeable about the client's medical condition.

39. Advocate with a psychiatric evaluator to also provide a physical examination.

40. Educate the client about the use and expected benefits of medication.

41. Monitor the client's medication compliance and effectiveness.

42. Review side effects of the medication with the client and the medical staff to identify a possible con-

founding influence of polypharmacy.

43. Monitor the client for permanent side effects of neuroleptic medications (e.g., tardive dyskinesia, muscle rigidity, dystonia).

44. Provide education to the client regarding precautions to take to avoid HIV infection and other STDs. Tailor this education to gender, sexual orientation, and specific mental illness groups to help shape his/her perspective of HIV risk.

45. Refer the client to a source for or provide him/her with condoms and clean-needle exchange programs.

46. Involve the client in peer education models to help him/her learn or educate others about HIV and other STD concerns.

47. Include the client's partner in outreach efforts regarding HIV and STD education.

48. Role-play assertiveness regarding implementing safer sex practices and other defenses for personal safety.

49. Educate the client and his/her partner and support system about the increased risk for physical, sexual, or domestic violence due to impaired functioning relative to psychosis and other severe and persistent mental illness symptoms.

50. Refer the client to a domestic violence support group.

51. Observe the family and the caregivers for frustrations that may reduce their ability to interact effectively with the client. Provide them with opportunities for venting their feelings.

52. Refer the caregivers to a support group for those who are affected by another's mental illness.

53. Teach the caregivers stress reduction techniques, such as muscle relaxation, abdominal breathing, and safe-place imagery.

54. Refer the client to a respite program to provide a brief rest from the demands of caring for a mentally ill patient.

—. _____
   _____

—. _____
   _____

—. _____
   _____

DIAGNOSTIC SUGGESTIONS

Axis I:	297.1	Delusional Disorder
	295.xx	Schizophrenia
	295.10	Schizophrenia, Disorganized Type
	295.30	Schizophrenia, Paranoid Type
	295.70	Schizoaffective Disorder
	296.xx	Bipolar I Disorder
	296.89	Bipolar II Disorder

293.0	Delirium Due to . . . [General Medical Condition]
294.xx	Dementia Due to . . . [General Medical Condition]
294.0	Amnestic Disorder Due to . . . [General Medical Condition]
333.xx	Neuroleptic-Related Syndromes
316	Psychological Factors Affecting a General Medical Condition
V62.89	Phase-of-Life Problem
_____	_____
_____	_____

HOMELESSNESS

BEHAVIORAL DEFINITIONS

1. A history of living on the streets on a sporadic or long-term basis.
2. Chronic periods during which the client does not maintain a permanent address.
3. Extensive utilization of shelters for the homeless, transitional housing, or other supported living placements.
4. Failure to make rent, mortgage, or utility payments, leading to a loss of residence.
5. Behavioral problems due to psychotic or other severe mental illness symptoms, resulting in eviction from residence.
6. Lack of knowledge regarding the basic skills that are needed to maintain a residence (e.g., cleaning, small repairs, budgeting).

—. _____
   _____
—. _____
   _____
—. _____
   _____

LONG-TERM GOALS

1. Movement from living on the street through a continuum of supported residential opportunities to a more stable independent residence.
2. Maintenance of a personal residence for an extended period of time.
3. Decreased dependence on transitional living programs or shelters for the homeless.

4. Acceptance and management of financial responsibilities as evidenced by paying bills on time.
5. Decreased behavioral concerns attained via stable medication use and supported by an increased level of motivation to stay healthy.
6. Understanding of basic residential skills, including budgeting, housecleaning, and social skills.

—. _____
_____

—. _____
_____

—. _____
_____

SHORT-TERM OBJECTIVES

1. Stabilize the current homelessness crisis. (1, 2, 3)
2. Describe the history of the homelessness. (4, 5)
3. Express emotions related to the homelessness. (5, 6, 7)
4. Verbalize fears regarding the attempts to obtain and maintain residence. (6, 7, 8, 9, 10)
5. Identify the barriers to maintaining long-term housing. (4, 5, 11, 12)
6. Stabilize the psychotic and other severe mental illness symptoms that interfere with maintaining a personal residence through the consistent use of psychotropic medication. (13, 14, 15)
7. Establish a mode of access to necessary medications

THERAPEUTIC INTERVENTIONS

1. Refer the client to a local shelter for the homeless.
2. Coordinate funds for a crisis residential placement (i.e., motel voucher or transitional program placement).
3. Facilitate the client's placement at the home of a family member, friend, or peer.
4. Request that the client describe his/her history of successful and problematic residential situations.
5. Direct the client to prepare a timeline of residences, periods of homelessness, and use of transitional housing. Process the factors contributing to his/her lifestyle.
6. Urge the client to identify feelings associated with the homeless situation.

despite the lack of a permanent residence or storage capacity. (13, 16, 17, 18)

8. Report the side effects and effectiveness of prescribed medications to an appropriate professional. (14, 15, 19)

9. Verbalize desires and expectations regarding long-term plans for residence. (20, 21)

10. Cooperate with behavioral, cognitive, and medical evaluations to assess readiness for independent living. (22, 23, 24)

11. Obtain funding for residence. (25, 26, 27)

12. Implement a budget and banking routine to facilitate the regular payment of rent or mortgage. (28, 29, 30)

13. Move from a more restrictive to a less restrictive housing setting. (20, 31, 32, 33)

14. Terminate substance abuse, which interferes with the ability to maintain housing. (34, 35, 36)

15. Obtain support from the family and peers to maintain housing. (3, 37, 38, 39, 40)

16. Demonstrate basic skills for running and maintaining a home or apartment. (28, 37, 41, 42, 43)

17. Develop plans to manage crises that could lead to destabilization and threaten residential status. (13, 44, 45, 46)

7. Provide the client with support and understanding regarding emotional concerns, acknowledging the natural emotions of frustration, discouragement, and embarrassment.

8. Explore possible fears associated with seeking a permanent residence, including fear of rejection, embarrassment, or failure.

9. Provide the client with realistic feedback regarding his/her paranoia or other irrational delusions.

10. Encourage the client to maintain important relationships at the homeless shelter when he/she moves to a more independent status.

11. Ask the client to describe specific barriers to maintaining housing.

12. Assist the client in negotiating the application process for desired housing programs.

13. Arrange for a psychiatric evaluation and for a prescription for psychotropic medication, if necessary.

14. Educate the client about the use, possible side effects, and expected benefits of medication.

15. Monitor the client's medication compliance.

16. Store medications for the client in a safe, easily accessible facility.

18. Reestablish residential housing quickly after recovering from decompensation. (31, 37, 47)

19. Verbalize an understanding of legal rights that are related to housing for the mentally disabled. (44, 48, 49, 50)

20. Increase independence as evidenced by involvement in a consumer-administered program. (38, 51, 52, 53)

—. _____
  _____

—. _____
  _____

—. _____
  _____

17. Provide the homeless client with smaller immediate supplies of medication.

18. Rent a secure storage space (e.g., locker or mailbox) in which the client may store necessary medications.

19. Monitor side effects of the medication with the client and inform the medical staff.

20. Educate the client about the available options regarding the continuum of supports and services that are available.

21. Guide the client in developing a list of pros and cons for each of the housing options; give structure for making his/her own decision regarding housing.

22. Assess the client for safety to himself/herself and to others.

23. Administer or refer the client for assessment of intellectual abilities as related to basic skills to maintain a home.

24. Coordinate a full medical evaluation to determine the client's physical care needs.

25. Assist the client with obtaining entitlements or other funding for general use.

26. Obtain specific subsidies that are available for assisting mentally ill individuals with housing.

27. Encourage and assist the client with obtaining regu-

lar employment to increase income that will defray housing costs. (See the Employment Problems chapter in this Planner.)

28. Assist the client in developing a budget for the payment of rent or mortgage. (See the Financial Needs chapter in this Planner.)

29. Assist the client in obtaining a low-interest, no-fee bank account with a participating bank.

30. Obtain emergency funds for payment of rent, mortgage, or utilities to prevent eviction.

31. Contact a discharge-planning coordinator of a state inpatient or a community psychiatric setting as early as possible in the client's treatment to coordinate discharge planning regarding housing.

32. Meet regularly with the incarcerated client to develop housing plans for after release.

33. Coordinate ample visitation to a new, less restrictive setting for the client to become acquainted with the setting; be readily available to the client for questions and reassurance.

34. Refer to AA, NA, or other substance abuse treatment options. (See the Chemical Dependence chapter in this Planner.)

35. Refer the client to a drug-free housing program.

36. Provide coordinated mental health and substance abuse services within a residential program or setting.

37. Encourage family members and friends to support and teach the client and to monitor his/her progress regarding basic living needs, medication administration, and financial management.

38. Refer the client to a support group for individuals with chronic mental illness.

39. Match the client with a mentor who has already successfully moved from homelessness to a stable living environment.

40. Transition the client to a brief respite placement in a more structured setting.

41. Teach the client basic housekeeping skills (e.g., see *Mary Ellen's Complete Home Reference Book* by Pinkham and Burg or *The Cleaning Encyclopedia: Your A to Z Illustrated Guide to Cleaning Like the Pros* by Aslett).

42. Refer the client to a structured program (within a continuum) to obtain hands-on training in basic skills for transitioning to more independent care.

43. Obtain visiting homemaker assistance for the client who

is not capable of doing such housekeeping activities.

44. Meet regularly with the housing manager to train about mental illness issues and the client's rights, to mitigate the client's problematic behaviors, and to assist in rent reviews and dwelling inspections.

45. Provide the housing manager with 24-hour access to the casemanager or the community mental health staff should emergencies arise.

46. Provide the client with an emergency health information card, including individualized information about who to call when in a crisis situation, including the casemanager and physicians.

47. Coordinate funds to maintain a client's residence when he/she is hospitalized or otherwise briefly loses eligibility for SSI benefits.

48. Train the client about his/her rights, as related to the Americans with Disabilities Act (ADA), including reasonable accommodations that must be made for them.

49. Educate the client about a tenant's rights (e.g., see *Renter's Rights* by Portman and Stewart).

50. Coordinate contact with legal assistance programs if the client's rights continue to be violated.

51. Refer the client to a consumer-administered housing program.

52. Assist the client in developing or participating in a consumer-administered business (e.g., cleaning crew, craft shop, snack service) to help maintain financial support.

53. Facilitate the client's involvement in consumer-administered programs, such as newsletters, mentoring, or agency committees.

__. _____
_____
__. _____
_____
__. _____
_____

DIAGNOSTIC SUGGESTIONS

Axis I:	297.1	Delusional Disorder
	295.xx	Schizophrenia
	295.10	Schizophrenia, Disorganized Type
	295.30	Schizophrenia, Paranoid Type
	295.90	Schizophrenia, Undifferentiated Type
	295.60	Schizophrenia, Residual Type
	295.70	Schizoaffective Disorder
	296.xx	Bipolar I Disorder
	296.89	Bipolar II Disorder
	V62.89	Phase-of-Life Problem
	_____	_____
	_____	_____

INDEPENDENT ACTIVITIES
OF DAILY LIVING (IADL)

BEHAVIORAL DEFINITIONS

1. Lack of access to, experience with, or functioning relative to independent activities of daily living [IADLs (e.g., transportation, banking, shopping, use of community services, or other skills that are necessary for living more independently)].
2. Anxiety regarding increasing IADLs.
3. Lack of knowledge of community resources.
4. Failure to respond appropriately in emergency situations.
5. Paranoia, psychosis, or other severe and persistent mental illness symptoms affect ability to use community resources independently.
6. Lack of familiarity with resources such as banking, stores, and other services.
7. Lack of attention to and organization of personal responsibilities, resulting in unpaid bills and unkept appointments.
8. Failure to access community resources such as worship centers, libraries, recreational areas, or businesses.
9. External restrictions placed on access to community resources due to bizarre behaviors.
10. History of others taking responsibility for performing IADLs for the client.

—. _____

_____

—. _____

_____

—. _____

_____

LONG-TERM GOALS

1. Increased knowledge of community resources.
2. Timely, appropriate, and safe responses to emergency situations.
3. Increased comfort with functioning independently.
4. Consistent use of available community resources.
5. Positive relationships with community resource providers.
6. Management of severe and persistent mental illness symptoms so as not to disturb others in the community.
7. Increased organization of and attention to daily routines, resulting in personal responsibilities being fulfilled.
8. Client takes responsibility for IADLs to level of own potential and develops resources for help from others.

—. _____
_____

—. _____
_____

—. _____
_____

SHORT-TERM OBJECTIVES

1. Describe current functioning in performing IADLs. (1, 2, 3)

2. Identify the barriers to increasing IADLs. (3, 4, 5)

3. Prioritize IADL areas upon which to focus effort and improve functioning. (1, 6, 7)

4. Identify any cognitive barriers to IADL success. (8)

5. Participate in a remediation program to teach IADL skills. (9)

6. Increase the frequency and appropriateness of social interaction. (10, 11, 12)

THERAPEUTIC INTERVENTIONS

1. Request that the client prepare an inventory of his/her positive and negative experiences with attempting to perform IADLs.

2. Ask the client to identify two areas in which he/she has experienced success in becoming more independent in the community.

3. Solicit from the client two areas in which he/she has experienced failure in becoming more independent.

4. Examine problematic IADL areas with the client to identify any patterns of be-

7. Develop and implement a regular schedule for performance of routine IADLs. (13, 14)

8. Acknowledge IADL deficits as a symptom of mental illness being inadequately controlled or treated. (15, 16)

9. Stabilize, through the use of psychotropic medications, psychotic and other severe and persistent mental illness symptoms that interfere with IADLs. (17, 18, 19)

10. Obtain and take prescribed medications on a regular basis. (18, 19, 20, 21, 22)

11. Report the side effects and the effectiveness of prescribed medications to the appropriate professional. (18, 19, 23)

12. Obtain the necessary transportation to work, medical appointments, leisure opportunities, or other desired destinations. (24, 25)

13. Use public transportation in a safe, socially appropriate, efficient manner. (26, 27, 28, 29)

14. Identify, attain, and manage adequate sources of financial income. (30, 31)

15. Use banking resources to facilitate financial independence. (28, 32, 33, 34, 35)

16. Utilize the services of a choice of stores in the community. (36, 37, 38)

17. Assert self to protect own rights against discrimina-

havior or cognitions that cause the failure at independent functioning.

5. Acquire the proper permission to release information, and obtain feedback from family members, friends, and caregivers about the client's performance of IADLs.

6. Ask the client to identify or describe those IADLs that are desired but not present in the current repertoire.

7. Assist the client in prioritizing IADLs and the skills that must be learned to implement these IADLs.

8. Refer the client for an assessment of cognitive abilities and deficits.

9. Recommend remediating programs to the client, such as skill-building groups, token economies, or behavior-shaping programs that are focused on removing deficits to IADL performance.

10. Explore the client's anxiety regarding social contacts and increasing independence.

11. Assist the client in learning the skills that are necessary for appropriate social behavior. (See the Social Skills chapter in this Planner.)

12. Provide positive feedback and encouragement to the client's attempts to increase social interaction.

tory barriers to community resources. (39, 40, 41)

18. Identify and process (negative) emotional responses to emergency service professionals. (42)

19. Use emergency service professionals effectively. (43, 44, 45, 46, 47)

20. Identify and contact alternative resources before contacting emergency response staff. (45, 48)

21. Enroll in education classes. (49)

22. Resolve problems with specific community businesses or service providers who have issued restrictions on access due to past inappropriate behavior. (3, 39, 50, 51, 52)

23. Request assistance from others when attempting to implement IADLs. (53, 54)

24. Agree to implement a specific plan to use when decompensating or when in crisis, relative to IADLs. (48, 55)

25. Increase involvement in recreational activities. (56, 57, 58, 59)

26. Participate in spiritual activities. (60, 61, 62)

13. Aid the client in developing a specific schedule for completing IADLs (e.g., arrange finances on Monday morning, go to the grocery store on Tuesday, etc.).

14. Teach the client about situations in which he/she should break from his/her established routine (e.g., do the banking on a different day due to a holiday, or do the weekly cleaning one day earlier to attend a desired social function).

15. Educate the client about the expected or common symptoms of his/her mental illness (e.g., manic excitement behaviors or negative symptoms of schizophrenia), which may negatively impact basic IADL functioning.

16. Reflect or interpret poor performance in IADLs as an indicator of psychiatric decompensation; share these observations with the client, the caregivers, and the medical staff.

17. Arrange for an evaluation of the client by a physician for a prescription for psychotropic medication.

18. Educate the client about the proper use and expected benefits of psychotropic medication.

19. Monitor the client for compliance with psychotropic medication that is prescribed and for its effective-

___. _____

_____

___. _____

_____

___. _____

_____

ness and possible side effects.

20. Review and model procedures for the procurement
of medications.

21. Develop an agreement with
the client regarding the
level of responsibility and
independence that he/she
must display to trigger a decrease in the clinician's
monitoring of medications.

22. Coordinate an agreement
between the client, the
pharmacist, and the clinician regarding circum-
stances that would trigger
the transfer of medication
monitoring back to the clinician (e.g., client's failure to
pick up monthly prescrip-
tion, client trying to refill a
prescription too soon, etc.).

23. Review the possible side effects of the medication with
the client and report any
significant incidence to the
medical staff.

24. Brainstorm possible transportation resources with the
client (e.g., public transportation, personal vehicle,
agency resources, friends
and family, walking, bicy-
cling, etc.).

25. Encourage and reinforce the
client's independent use of
transportation resources.

26. Familiarize the client with
available public transportation options through discussion, written schedules, and

accompanied use of community services.

27. Review the typical expectations for using public transportation, including payment, time schedule, and social norms for behavior.

28. Predict possible influences that the client's severe and persistent mental illness symptoms may have on his/her ability to use community services. Help the client brainstorm techniques to decrease these symptom effects (e.g., relaxation techniques, escape/ avoidance plans, graduated steps to independence, etc.).

29. Ride with the client to various destinations on public transportation until he/she is adequately comfortable with doing so alone.

30. Assist the client in identifying and attaining adequate sources of income. (See the Employment Problems and the Financial Needs chapters in this Planner.)

31. Develop a budget with the client that is based on resources and needs. (See the Financial Needs chapter in this Planner.)

32. Review the procedures for and the advantages of using the banking system to assist the client with IADLs, including increased security, financial organization, and

convenience for paying bills;
caution the client about the
hazards that are related to
banking (e.g., credit debt,
overdrawn checking account
charges, etc.).

33. Coordinate a helping relationship between specific
bank staff and the client.
With a proper permission to
release information, provide
information to the bank
staff about the client's
needs and disabilities.

34. Encourage the client to use
a specific staff at a specific
bank branch to develop a
more personal and under-
standing relationship.

35. Coordinate an agreement
between the client, a specified bank staff, and a
clinician regarding the circumstances under which
the clinician should be noti-
fied (e.g., manic client attempts to withdraw his/her
entire savings account).

36. Familiarize the client with
commercial resources that
are available in his/her area
through a review of news-
paper advertisements and a
tour of the business dis-
tricts in the community.

37. Role-play situations that
commonly occur while shopping at a store (e.g., asking
for assistance, declining a
pushy salesperson, returning a defective item, etc.).
Provide the client with feed-

back about his/her functioning in these situations.

38. Go with the client to businesses at which he/she is
uncomfortable or uncertain,
gradually decreasing sup-
port.

39. Support the client in his/her
assertive response to in-
stances of discrimination
due to mental illness symptoms.

40. Advocate for the client with
area businesses or service
providers who restrict access due to concern over
mental illness symptoms.

41. Link the client to advocacy
and support groups that
will assist in developing
open access for the client to
community businesses and
services.

42. Explore the client's prior
contact with emergency response professionals. Help
the client identify situations
in which emergency re-
sponse staff were required to
coerce the client (e.g., a prior
involuntary hospitalization),
as well as when the client
may have manipulated
emergency response staff
(e.g., threatened harm to
himself/herself for some secondary gain such as obtaining food or a place to sleep).

43. Develop a list of specific
emergency response professionals who respond effectively to mentally ill

individuals (e.g., a police unit mental health liaison or a specific nurse/orderly at the emergency room). Direct the client to seek out that professional when he/she contacts that agency or facility. Maintain regular contact with the identified professionals.

44. Provide 24-hour crisis consultation to all emergency response professionals to assist in responding to the client's use of emergency systems.

45. Teach the client the appropriate use of specific emergency service professionals, including their responsibilities and limitations.

46. Provide the client with easy-to-read lists of emergency numbers.

47. Provide the client in crisis who does not have access to a telephone with a cellular phone that is preprogrammed to call only to a 24-hour crisis line.

48. Brainstorm alternative resources that are available to the client for use instead of "nuisance" calls to emergency response staff (e.g., contact a crisis line for psychotic symptom development, contact a support group member when lonely instead of going to the emergency room, contact family first if feeling ill, etc.).

49. Coordinate the client's enrollment in continuing education, Graduate Equivalency Degree (GED) classes, or college courses.

50. Discuss the need for making amends to businesses or service providers who have been affected by the client's past inappropriate behavior.

51. Brainstorm with the client about the form of restitution (an apology, a service provided, or financial reimbursement).

52. Help the client develop a specific plan for how to implement restitution (e.g., how to approach the business owner, what service could be offered in restitution, where the client will get the money to pay the business owner for debt, etc.).

53. Ask the client to identify a list of personal resources that he/she can use for assistance in carrying out IADLs (e.g., family and friends, support group members, neighbors, etc.).

54. Role-play how to approach strangers for basic assistance (e.g., asking for directions). Provide feedback to the client about his/her approach, personal hygiene or dress, and how appearance and manner affect the stranger's comfort level. (See the Activities of Daily

Living and the Social Skills chapters in this Planner.)

55. Assist the client in developing a written plan with telephone numbers of resources and clinical assistance for use when he/she is at risk of decompensation.

56. Refer the client to an activity therapist for an assessment of recreational needs, skills, and opportunities.

57. Assist the client in identifying a variety of recreational activities in which he/she might be interested. Provide the client with information that is related to the accessibility of these activities.

58. Shadow the client to provide support while he/she attends chosen activities. Allow the client to determine how closely the clinician is involved to decrease stigma and to increase independent functioning.

59. Coordinate a mentor program so the client can have an identified individual who assists him/her in becoming comfortable with the recreational/social setting.

60. Explore the client's interest in involvement in spiritual activities.

61. Acknowledge to the client the potential for his/her confusion regarding spiritual messages and imagery; assist in differentiating between spiritual concerns

and symptoms of mental illness.

62. Coordinate the client's attendance at his/her pre-
ferred place of worship.

——. _____
_____

——. _____
_____

——. _____
_____

DIAGNOSTIC SUGGESTIONS

Axis I: 297.1   Delusional Disorder
295.xx   Schizophrenia
295.10   Schizophrenia, Disorganized Type
295.30   Schizophrenia, Paranoid Type
295.90   Schizophrenia, Undifferentiated Type
295.60   Schizophrenia, Residual Type
295.70   Schizoaffective Disorder
296.xx   Bipolar I Disorder
296.89   Bipolar II Disorder

_____   _____
_____   _____

INTIMATE RELATIONSHIP CONFLICTS

BEHAVIORAL DEFINITIONS

1. Indifferent to the emotional needs of the partner.
2. Distrust of partner due to paranoia or other severe and persistent mental illness symptoms.
3. Increased levels of stress in the relationship due to the effects of erratic behavior (e.g., legal problems, impulsive spending, inability to work).
4. A pattern of repeated separations and/or divorce or discontinuation of relationships due to personal deficiencies in problem solving, social skills, or assertion.
5. Impulsive sexual involvement outside of the committed relationship.
6. Increased spousal discontent with the changes in the relationship due to the severe and persistent mental illness symptom.
7. Violent or abusive interactions between partners.

__. _____
   _____
__. _____
   _____
__. _____
   _____

LONG-TERM GOALS

1. Decrease the severe and persistent mental illness symptoms that affect the relationship.
2. Increase understanding of the effects of mental illness symptoms on the relationship.

3. Develop a more trusting relationship with partner.
4. Develop techniques for reducing stress in the relationship.
5. Maintain the relationship despite problems related to severe and persistent mental illness symptoms.
6. Preserve fidelity within the relationship by discontinuing impulsive sexual acting out.
7. Process changes in the relationship that have occurred as a result of the chronic mental illness.
8. Increase relationship skills such as problem solving, assertion, or social skills.
9. Resolve problems without verbal or physical abuse.

—. _____
   _____
—. _____
   _____
—. _____
   _____

SHORT-TERM OBJECTIVES

1. Describe the history of intimate relationship concerns. (1, 2, 3, 4)
2. Identify the status of the current relationship. (3, 5, 6)
3. Partner and client to acknowledge how the severe and persistent mental illness symptoms affect the relationship. (7, 8, 9)
4. Cooperate with a referral to a physician for a psychotropic medication evaluation. (10)
5. Report a decrease in mental illness symptoms that affect the relationship through the regular use of psychiatric medications. (10, 11, 12, 13)

THERAPEUTIC INTERVENTIONS

1. Explore the client's history of intimate relationships, including positive and negative outcomes.
2. Use a graphic display, such as a timeline, to display the client's history of intimate relationship concerns. Help the client to identify additional key portions of the timeline, such as the onset of symptoms or treatment.
3. Obtain feedback from the client's partner about the history of their relationship conflicts.
4. Ask the extended family for feedback about the client's

6. Report the side effects and effectiveness of the medications to the appropriate professional. (11, 12, 14)

7. Enlist and cooperate with partner support in monitoring the medication prescription compliance. (11, 13, 15, 16)

8. Partner to verbalize an understanding of techniques for coping with severe and persistent mental illness symptoms in a loved one. (7, 17, 18, 19)

9. Partner to share his/her feelings related to the client's mental illness symptoms. (20, 21, 22)

10. Partner to list relationships, activities, and interests outside of those with the client that provide some diversion, respite, and balance to life. (23)

11. Partner to attend a support group for the family and friends of individuals with severe mental illness. (24)

12. Express feelings about the onset of severe mental illness symptoms. (25)

13. Implement newly acquired communication skills in the relationship. (26, 27)

14. Partner and the client to verbalize increased trust in the relationship. (28, 29, 30)

15. Identify role changes in the relationship that are due to mental illness. (31, 32, 33)

history of relationship successes and problems.

5. Request that the client identify successes and challenges in his/her current relationship.

6. Coordinate the administration of marital satisfaction surveys (e.g., *The Marital Satisfaction Inventory* by Snyder or *The Marital Status Inventory* by Weiss and Correto).

7. Educate the client and his/her partner about the common symptoms of the client's mental illness; recommend books for further information (e.g., *Schizophrenia: The Facts* by Tsuang and Faraone or *Bipolar Disorder: A Guide for Patients and Families* by Mondimore).

8. Request that the client (and partner) identify at least two ways in which the relationship has been affected by the severe and persistent mental illness symptoms.

9. Emphasize the fact that neither the family nor the partner are the cause of the client's mental illness.

10. Arrange for an evaluation by a physician for a prescription for psychotropic medication.

11. Educate the client (and his/her significant other) about the use and expected benefits of the medication.

16. Client and partner to identify the level of closeness/distance desired in the relationship, and how this may vary due to symptoms. (29, 34, 35)

17. Terminate substance use or abuse. (36, 37)

18. Increase sexual functioning by eliminating physiological problems. (38, 39)

19. Improve personal appearance related to sexual arousal. (40)

20. Partner and the client read books and/or watch educational videos regarding human sexuality. (41)

21. Verbalize an understanding of the need for a positive emotional climate which increases desire for sexual intimacy. (5, 35, 40, 42)

22. Acknowledge a history of sexual acting out and the negative effect it has had on the relationship with this partner. (43, 44, 45)

23. Partner to share his/her feelings related to the client's sexual acting out. (45)

24. Verbalize an agreement on appropriate sexual, emotional, and social boundaries with others (e.g., acceptable and unacceptable sexual or emotional contact). (46)

25. Implement anger control techniques. (47, 48)

12. Monitor the client's medication compliance and effectiveness.

13. Obtain feedback from the partner regarding the client's medication compliance and efficacy.

14. Review the possible side effects of the medications with the client and the medical staff to identify the client's side effects or the confounding influence of polypharmacy.

15. Coordinate an agreement with the client and his/her partner about the responsibility for administration and monitoring of the medication.

16. Develop specific plans for the circumstances under which control of the medication will be returned to the client (e.g., extended period of time in remission).

17. Assign the client's partner to read books on coping with a loved one who has a severe and persistent mental illness (e.g., *When Someone You Love Has a Mental Illness* by Woolis, *Surviving Schizophrenia: A Manual for Families, Consumers, and Providers* by Torrey, or *Bipolar Puzzle Solution: A Mental Health Client's Perspective* by Court and Nelson).

18. Teach the partner specific techniques to help manage

26. Agree to a safety plan to prevent any future abuse of family members. (48, 49)

27. Generate mutually agreeable strategies for parenting. (48, 49, 50, 51, 52)

28. Report a decrease in marital stress due to stabilizing financial concerns. (53, 54)

29. Process emotions regarding the end of this relationship. (55, 56, 57)

30. Attend a support group for individuals with severe and persistent mental illness. (57)

—. _____

_____

—. _____

_____

—. _____

_____

the client when he/she is agitated, psychotic, or manic (e.g., maintaining a calm demeanor, providing basic directives, redirection). (See the Psychosis or the Mania/Hypomania chapters in this Planner.)

19. Role-play calm, assertive responses to psychotic behaviors with the client's partner.

20. Process the partner's emotional reaction to the client's onset or recurrence of severe and persistent mental illness.

21. Reassure the client's partner about how accessible the clinician will be for consultation, questions, or support.

22. Provide the client's partner with telephone numbers to 24-hour crisis lines for professional assistance when the clinician is not available.

23. Emphasize the need for the partner and all family members to have interests outside of the mental illness concerns that the client may present.

24. Refer the client's partner to a support group for the family and friends of the mentally ill.

25. Assist the client in expressing his/her feelings regarding experiencing severe and persistent mental illness symptoms and how these affect the relationship.

26. Facilitate conjoint sessions with the client's partner, focusing on increasing relational communication and learning problem-solving skills.

27. Teach the client and his/her partner specific skills for communication, such as expressing specific positive and negative emotions, making requests, communicating information clearly, giving "I" messages, and implementing active listening.

28. Focus the client and his/her partner on identifying trust issues that are attributable to mental illness symptoms such as paranoia or mania. Emphasize the nonvolitional aspects of these symptoms.

29. Explore each partner's fears regarding getting too close and feeling vulnerable to hurt, rejection, or abandonment.

30. Request that the client and his/her partner identify specific areas in which they have experienced increased trust. Focus on ways to generalize this trust into other areas.

31. Request that the client and his/her partner identify the changes that have occurred in the relationship due to the client's mental illness symptoms.

32. Challenge the couple to identify the ways in which

power and control can be shared despite mental illness symptoms (e.g., develop advanced directives regarding treatment expectations, returning responsibilities to the mentally ill partner during periods of stabilization, etc.).

33. Legitimize the client's and partner's need to mourn the loss of functioning in the relationship, or the changes that have occurred due to the severe and persistent mental illness symptoms.

34. Facilitate a discussion of the factors that contribute to the desire for closeness or distance/safety.

35. Acknowledge the normal need for the client's partner to have a "waiting period" after the client's symptoms have abated prior to resuming normal levels of trust, interaction, sexual activity, and so forth.

36. Explore the role of substance abuse as a potentiating factor for the client's severe and persistent mental illness symptoms as well as relationship problems.

37. Coordinate providing the client with integrated substance abuse and mental health treatment. (See the Chemical Dependence chapter in this Planner.)

38. Refer the client to a physician for a complete physical

examination to rule out or to identify any physiological or medication-related barriers to sexual functioning.

39. Coordinate follow-up on recommendations from a physician (e.g., medications, specialty assessments, or lab work). Inform the treating psychiatrist about sexual dysfunction concerns, physical exam, and follow-up needs.

40. Focus the client on physical appearance and personal hygiene needs as a sexual arousal issue for his/her partner. (See the Activities of Daily Living chapter in this Planner.)

41. Direct the client and his/her intimate partner to read books on human sexual functioning (e.g., *The New Joy of Sex* by Comfort or *The Reader's Digest Guide to Love and Sex* by Roberts and Padgett-Yawn) and/or to watch sex educational videos (e.g., *Better Sex Videos* by the Sinclair Institute).

42. Emphasize to the client the concept of the sexual relationship being a mirror of the rest of the relationship, and the need for positive emotional interaction prior to sexual involvement.

43. Identify the history of (impulsive) sexual acting out and the effect it has had in the relationship.

44. Assist the manic or impulsive client in managing symptoms. (See the Mania/Hypomania chapter in this Planner.)

45. Process the partner's emotions related to the client's history of infidelity.

46. Assist the partners in developing a clear set of boundaries for sexual, emotional, and social contact with others.

47. Teach the client about anger control techniques. (See the Anger Management chapter in this Planner.)

48. Develop a time-out signal to be used when either partner becomes fearful that abuse may occur to anyone in the family.

49. Develop safety plans, including when public safety officers should be contacted, or how to utilize domestic violence services.

50. Assist the couple in identifying how mental illness symptoms affect the children in the relationship (e.g., confusion, embarrassment, caretaking).

51. Educate the parents about effective child-rearing practices (e.g., see *1-2-3 Magic: Effective Discipline for Children 2–12, Second Edition,* by Phelan).

52. Facilitate an agreement regarding acceptable parent-

ing practices, which should include issues such as discipline and rewards, or when the partner should become involved. (See the Parenting chapter in this Planner.)

53. Assist the client in obtaining work (see the Employment Problems chapter in this Planner) or other sources of income, such as disability payments (see the Financial Needs chapter in this Planner).

54. Refer the client and his/her intimate partner for credit counseling or other budgeting assistance.

55. Encourage the client to express his/her emotions regarding the loss of this relationship.

56. Assign the client to read portions of *How to Survive the Loss of a Love* by Colgrove, Bloomfield, and McWilliams; process contents.

57. Refer the client to a support group for individuals with mental illness concerns.

—. _____

_____

—. _____

_____

—. _____

_____

DIAGNOSTIC SUGGESTIONS

Axis I:
297.1	Delusional Disorder
295.xx	Schizophrenia
295.10	Schizophrenia, Disorganized Type
295.30	Schizophrenia, Paranoid Type
295.90	Schizophrenia, Undifferentiated Type
295.60	Schizophrenia, Residual Type
295.70	Schizoaffective Disorder
296.xx	Bipolar I Disorder
296.89	Bipolar II Disorder
V61.1	Partner Relational Problem
V61.9	Relational Problem Related to a Mental Disorder
V62.81	Relational Problem NOS
_____	_____
_____	_____

LEGAL CONCERNS

BEHAVIORAL DEFINITIONS

1. A pattern of illegal behavior, including theft, assault, disorderly conduct, or threats to others.
2. A history of arrests, convictions, and incarceration due to illegal behaviors.
3. Current legal involvement, including pending charges, incarceration, or probation/parole oversight.
4. Difficulty functioning in a corrections setting due to paranoia, mania, or other severe and persistent mental illness symptoms.
5. Vulnerability to attack or manipulation by others while incarcerated.
6. Illegal behaviors related to substance use or abuse (e.g., drunk driving, drug possession).
7. Guardianship dictated by the courts.
8. The pursuit of the court naming a legal guardian by clinicians, family members, or others.
9. Imminent threat of harm to self or others due to mental illness symptoms, resulting in involuntary court-ordered hospitalization.
10. A need for legal representation due to arrests, involuntary hospitalization, guardianship procedures, or advocacy.
11. Inappropriate loss of basic personal rights due to a lack of advocacy.

__. _____

_____

__. _____

_____

__. _____

_____

LONG-TERM GOALS

1. Terminate illegal behaviors by utilizing legal means to meet needs.
2. Decrease inappropriate arrest or incarceration due to behaviors that are related to mental health symptoms.
3. Accept responsibility for decisions or behaviors that have resulted in arrest, arraignment, or trial.
4. Obtain competent, caring legal representation for criminal, civil, or probate matters.
5. Decrease mental illness symptoms and/or substance abuse, which prompt illegal activity or involuntary hospitalization.
6. Obtain the least restrictive, most appropriate guardianship status.
7. Advocate for basic personal rights, such as the freedom to live, work, or play in chosen areas.
8. Complete incarceration, probation, or parole successfully.
9. Maintain safety while incarcerated.

__. _____
_____
_____
__. _____
_____
_____
__. _____
_____

SHORT-TERM OBJECTIVES

1. Describe the behaviors or symptoms that have led to legal involvement. (1, 2, 3, 4)
2. Identify current criminal charges and legal needs. (2, 4, 5, 6)
3. Verbalize an understanding of the legal system as it relates to current legal or criminal charges. (7, 8)
4. Participate in a complete forensic evaluation to assess criminal responsibility/safety. (9, 10)

THERAPEUTIC INTERVENTIONS

1. Request that the client identify his/her history of illegal behaviors and the legal system's responses.
2. Obtain a copy of the client's criminal history. Compare the record with his/her disclosed history, inquiring about discrepancies.
3. Review a copy of the client's guardianship stipulations with him/her, and why they are in place.

5. Present a positive impression in the court setting. (11, 12, 13, 14, 15)

6. Participate in an evaluation by a physician as to the need for medication to treat severe and persistent mental illness symptoms. (16, 17, 18)

7. Report side effects and effectiveness of psychotropic medications to the appropriate professional. (17, 18, 19)

8. Successfully complete jail sentence. (20, 21, 22, 23, 24)

9. Remain safe while incarcerated. (23, 25, 26, 27)

10. Successfully complete probation or other sentencing requirements that have been set forth by the court. (28, 29, 30)

11. Family and support system assist the client through the legal system. (31, 32, 33)

12. Take responsibility for illegal behaviors. (1, 34, 35, 36)

13. Decrease mental illness symptoms that contribute to illegal behavior. (16, 17, 37, 38)

14. Terminate substance use or abuse. (39, 40)

15. Participate in a psychological evaluation regarding guardianship. (41)

16. Obtain the least restrictive, legally necessary guardianship. (42, 43, 44, 45)

17. Execute a last will and testament. (6, 45, 46)

4. Assess the client for a pattern of antisocial behavior.

5. Obtain specific information regarding current legal charges, such as police reports, court documents, or attorney reports.

6. Assist the client in making decisions about the need for legal representation. Refer the client to an attorney, if necessary.

7. Review the basic proceedings and the people who are involved in a court hearing. Quiz the client about the role of each person to test his/her understanding.

8. Display the steps in a criminal proceeding graphically, identifying the reason for each step in the process (e.g., investigation, arrest, arraignment, pretrial conferences, trial, and sentencing).

9. Arrange for a complete psychological assessment of the client's functioning, including intellectual, cognitive, and personality testing, to assess the client's understanding of criminal behaviors.

10. Advocate for a forensic evaluation through the court system to assess the client's fitness to stand trial.

11. Coach the client in preparations for court hearings, such as doing personal grooming, clothing selec-

18. Verbalize an understanding of all legal rights and responsibilities regarding treatment. (47, 48, 49)

19. Identify parenting responsibilities, strengths, and deficits. (49, 50, 51)

__. _____
_____

__. _____
_____

__. _____
_____

tion, and gathering appropriate documentation.

12. Review normal conventions in a court setting with the client (e.g., referring to the judge as "Your Honor," standing when the judge enters, and waiting for the appropriate time to speak).

13. Instruct the client about how to be a good witness (e.g., tell the truth, only answer the question asked, be prepared for an opposing attorney to try to increase his/her anxiety).

14. Role-play a court hearing, emphasizing the progression of the hearing, typical conventions in the courtroom, and being a witness.

15. Attend court hearings with the client, providing emotional support and reassurance.

16. Refer the client to a physician or a psychiatrist for an evaluation of the need for psychiatric medication.

17. Educate the client about the use and expected benefits of psychiatric medications.

18. Monitor the client's medication compliance and effectiveness.

19. Review side effects of the medications with the client and the medical staff.

20. With the client's permission, advise the jail staff about the client's mental illness symptoms. Provide the

jail staff with information and training regarding how to work with the client.

21. Advocate with the court and the jail system for alternative sentencing/housing options for the client as a mentally ill offender who is unable to cope with the typical jail setting (e.g., tether, a mental health unit of the jail).

22. Assist the client in developing an understanding of how his/her mental illness symptoms may interact with incarceration (e.g., increased paranoia, more acute anxiety, or difficulty managing mania).

23. Contact a specific person within the legal system who will provide regular advocacy for the mentally ill inmate (e.g., a mental health liaison).

24. Monitor the provision of medication in the corrections setting. Advise the jail staff of the potential side effects that they should be monitoring, as well as the potential danger resulting from neglecting the client's medications.

25. Review personal safety considerations with the client while he/she is incarcerated (e.g., how other inmates may treat him/her, how to get help if threatened or assaulted, how to respond to others).

26. Assist the client in identifying assertive, nonviolent responses to potentially hostile individuals in a jail setting.

27. Maintain contact with the client during his/her incarceration to provide support and to allow the client to vent about stressors in the jail setting to decrease his/her acting out.

28. Monitor, facilitate, and encourage the client to keep appointments with the court officers.

29. Attend probation meetings with the client on an intermittent basis to facilitate communication. Educate the probation staff about the client's strengths and limitations.

30. Support or facilitate the client's involvement in court-mandated activities to adhere to probation requirements (e.g., mental health treatment, job procurement, stable residence, community service).

31. Educate the client's family, friends, and caregivers about the legal system.

32. Encourage the client's family, friends, and caregivers to allow the client to experience the appropriate legal ramification of his/her inappropriate behavior (i.e., incarceration if the client was not actively psychotic and

mandatory hospitalization if psychosis is uncontrolled).

33. Challenge the client's support system to remain in contact with the client, despite his/her incarceration.

34. Request that the client identify ways in which his/her illegal behaviors have affected others. Help the client to empathize by identifying his/her own emotional responses to prior experiences of being victimized.

35. Encourage the client to provide restitution to those whom he/she has victimized (e.g., financial reimbursement or community service).

36. Assist the client in clarifying the values that allow illegal actions versus those values that do not.

37. Assist the client in developing an understanding of how his/her mental illness symptoms contribute to illegal behaviors.

38. Refer the client to individual, group, or marital therapy to assist in developing alternatives to acting out when facing stressful circumstances.

39. Coordinate a substance abuse evaluation with an individual/agency that is familiar with chronic mental illness concerns.

40. Provide coordinated mental health/substance abuse treatment. (See the Chemi-

cal Dependence chapter in this Planner.)

41. Coordinate a psychological evaluation to facilitate a guardianship hearing, including an assessment of functional decision-making abilities (e.g., regarding treatment, finances, etc.).

42. Assist the family members or other parties in obtaining guardianship of the client to increase supervision and monitoring of his/her behavior and treatment.

43. Educate the potential guardian about issues related to person-centered planning and the ability of mentally ill people to manage many aspects of their lives despite serious and persistent symptoms.

44. Advocate for the client against unnecessary or overly restrictive guardianship orders or practices.

45. Assist the client in developing a written description of his/her wishes for treatment, emergency contact, medication needs, and other issues should he/she decompensate and become unable legally to make such decisions.

46. Discuss the client's wishes for end-of-life issues, including funeral arrangements, estate dispersal, and financial needs.

47. Advise the client (both verbally and in writing) about his/her legal rights regarding treatment (e.g., confidentiality, informed consent, refusal of services).

48. Focus the client on his/her responsibilities regarding treatment (e.g., attendance at appointments, providing the clinician with accurate information, confidentiality regarding other patients in treatment).

49. Advocate for the client with other clinicians, family members, and legal personnel to adhere to the client's rights.

50. Clarify with the client his/her parenting abilities, responsibilities, and needs for assistance.

51. Assist the client in developing increased parenting skills. (See the Parenting chapter in this Planner.)

__. _____
    _____

__. _____
    _____

__. _____
    _____

DIAGNOSTIC SUGGESTIONS

Axis I:	297.1	Delusional Disorder
	295.xx	Schizophrenia
	295.10	Schizophrenia, Disorganized Type

295.20   Schizophrenia, Catatonic Type
295.90   Schizophrenia, Undifferentiated Type
295.30   Schizophrenia, Paranoid Type
295.70   Schizoaffective Disorder
296.xx   Bipolar I Disorder
296.89   Bipolar II Disorder
297.1   Delusional Disorder
304.20   Cocaine Dependence
303.90   Alcohol Dependence
312.30   Kleptomania
V71.01   Adult Antisocial Behavior

_____   _____

_____   _____

Axis II: 301.7   Antisocial Personality Disorder

_____   _____

_____   _____

MANIA/HYPOMANIA

BEHAVIORAL DEFINITIONS

1. Loquaciousness or pressured speech.
2. Flight of ideas or reports of thoughts racing.
3. Bizarre, delusional, grandiose, or persecutory beliefs or actions.
4. Physiological changes, including a decreased need for sleep or a highly variable appetite.
5. Psychomotor agitation, restlessness, or agitation.
6. Exacerbated loss of natural inhibitions leading to impulsive, self-gratifying behaviors, regardless of the consequences to self or others (e.g., buying sprees, substance abuse).
7. Expansive, variable mood that leads to impatience, irritability, anger, or assaultiveness when thwarted or confronted.
8. Failure to follow through on projects or promises due to an inability to organize an activity in a goal-directed manner.
9. Behaviors that show a disregard for social mores (e.g., public nudity, erratic driving).

—. _____
   _____

—. _____
   _____

—. _____
   _____

LONG-TERM GOALS

1. Reduce psychological energy and return to premorbid levels of activity, judgment, mood, and goal-directed behavior.

2. Control erratic behaviors, with an increased understanding and sensitivity regarding how behavior affects others.
3. Express emotions regarding how severe and persistent mental illness symptoms affect self-esteem, developing healthy coping skills for these emotions.
4. Achieve a more reality-based orientation.
5. Stabilize sleeping pattern and appetite.
6. Increase goal-directed behaviors.
7. Develop an increased understanding of severe and persistent mental illness symptoms, as well as an understanding of the indicators of and the triggers for decompensation.

—. _____
_____
_____

—. _____
_____
_____

—. _____
_____
_____

SHORT-TERM OBJECTIVES

1. Describe feelings and thoughts about self, own abilities, and future plans. (1, 2)

2. Accept placement in an environment that ensures safety to self and others. (2, 3, 4)

3. Maintain community placement while managing manic episode. (2, 3, 5, 6, 7)

4. Describe mood state, energy level, sleeping pattern, and amount of control over thoughts. (1, 2, 8, 9)

5. Participate in an evaluation by a physician as to the need for medication to treat

THERAPEUTIC INTERVENTIONS

1. Monitor the client for classic signs of mania: pressured speech, impulsive behavior, euphoric mood, flight of ideas, reduced need for sleep, inflated self-esteem, and high energy level.

2. Assess the client's current stage of euphoria: none, hypomanic, manic, or psychotic.

3. Perform an assessment of the client's ability to remain safe in the community, including level of manic behavior, impulsivity, natural and programmatic supports, and access to potentially unsafe situations.

severe and persistent mental illness symptoms. (10, 11, 12)

6. Report the side effects and the effectiveness of psychotropic medications to the appropriate professional. (11, 12, 13)

7. Verbalize an increased understanding of severe and persistent mental illness symptoms and causes. (14, 15)

8. Identify the triggers and indicators of manic episodes. (8, 14, 16, 17)

9. Express the emotions that are related to losses that have been experienced due to severe and persistent mental illness symptoms. (18, 19)

10. Express the fears that are related to a recurrence of symptoms. (18, 20)

11. Express a sense of self-control over illness and life circumstances. (17, 21, 22, 23)

12. Maintain a reality-based orientation. (12, 17, 24, 25, 26)

13. Identify and discontinue unhealthy or self-destructive behaviors early in the decompensation process. (8, 17, 27, 28, 29)

14. Develop a calm, serene level of activity. (7, 10, 30, 31, 32)

15. Obtain a normal level of sleep (5 to 8 hours per night, 5 of 7 nights per week). (10, 33, 34, 35)

4. Arrange for admission into a crisis residential unit or psychiatric hospital if the client is judged to be at imminent risk of harm to himself/herself or to others.

5. Develop a short-term, round-the-clock crisis plan, including multiple caregivers, psychiatric involvement, and crisis assistance, to maintain the client within the community.

6. Remove potentially dangerous items, such as sharp objects, weapons, and access to motor vehicles.

7. Provide the client with a calm setting, including low lighting; decreased stimulation (e.g., soothing music); and a direct, but nonargumentative, approach.

8. Obtain feedback from the family, friends, and caregivers of the client regarding his/her mood, energy level, and sleeping and eating patterns.

9. Request the client to identify his/her current level of mood, energy level, control over thoughts, and sleeping pattern.

10. Refer the client to a physician or a psychiatrist for an evaluation of the need for psychiatric medication (e.g., mood stabilizers such as lithium carbonate or Depakote).

16. Establish regular eating habits and nutritional intake. (10, 36, 37, 38)

17. Decrease or ameliorate the direct effects of hostile, promiscuous, or otherwise impulsive manic behaviors. (39, 40)

18. Reestablish relationships that have been broken due to the effects of severe and persistent mental illness symptoms. (15, 41, 42, 43)

19. Family members and other supportive people increase their contact with and assistance to the client. (8, 15, 44)

20. Verbalize an understanding of the long-standing nature of severe and persistent mental illness and commit self to ongoing treatment. (14, 15, 45, 46, 47)

—. _____
   _____

—. _____
   _____

—. _____
   _____

11. Educate the client about the use and expected benefits of psychiatric medications.

12. Monitor the client's medication compliance and effectiveness.

13. Review side effects of the medications with the client and the medical staff.

14. Educate the client about typical symptoms and causes of mania and hypomania.

15. Refer the client and his/her family and friends to written materials, such as *Bipolar Puzzle Solution: A Mental Health Client's Perspective* by Court and Nelson, *Surviving Schizophrenia: A Family Manual* by Torrey, or *Bipolar Disorder: A Guide for Patients and Families* by Mondimore.

16. Explore the stressors that may have precipitated the client's manic behaviors (e.g., school/work failure, social rejection, or family trauma).

17. Direct the client to prepare a written list of behavioral indicators of the start of a manic episode (e.g., difficulty sleeping, urge to spend impulsively, irritability). Assist the client in providing this information to his/her support system.

18. Refer the client to a therapist for individual or group treatment regarding loss issues.

19. Explore the client's experience of and fears of abandonment and stigmatization, providing empathy and support.

20. Inquire about the client's fear of decompensation and recurrence of symptoms; reassure the client regarding successful treatment and the support system that is available to provide care and protection, if necessary.

21. Use person-centered planning principles and include the client in all areas of treatment planning and implementation.

22. Encourage and facilitate situations in which the client can exert self-control, such as taking increased responsibility in specified areas (e.g., medication, cooking, etc.).

23. Assist the client in developing long- and short-term goals (e.g., maintain medications, contact one friend, apply for work) that are attainable and realistic.

24. Help the client to differentiate between real and imagined, actual and exaggerated losses, abilities, and expectations.

25. Confront the client's grandiosity and demandingness gradually but firmly.

26. Interpret the fear and insecurity underlying the client's

braggadocio, hostility, and denial of dependency.

27. Refocus the client consistently onto the effects of his/her actions, emphasizing the impulsive nature of manic/hypomanic episodes and his/her need to identify these symptoms as early as possible.

28. Increase the client's sensitivity to the effects of his/her behavior through the use of role playing, role reversal, and behavioral rehearsal.

29. Identify and confront unhealthy, impulsive, or manic behaviors that occur during contacts with the clinician, enforcing clear rules and roles in the relationship, as well as immediate, short-term consequences for breaking such boundaries.

30. Teach the client relaxation and breathing techniques, such as those in *The Relaxation and Stress Reduction Workbook, Fourth Edition,* by Davis, Eshelman, and McKay.

31. Assist the client in setting limits on his/her own behavior, providing him/her with feedback and support.

32. Verbally reinforce increased relaxation and control over impulsivity and restlessness.

33. Teach the client effective sleep hygiene techniques (e.g., *No More Sleepless*

Nights: A Proven Guide to Conquering Insomnia by Hauri and Linde or *Good Nights: How to Stop Sleep Deprivation, Overcome Insomnia, and Get the Sleep You Need* by Zammit and Zanca.

34. Provide a sleep documentation chart to the client or the caregiver to identify patterns of sleep. Present this feedback to the client.

35. Encourage the client to practice a regular routine, including daily exercise and specific bedtime routines.

36. Monitor the client's food intake, noting consumption of caffeine, spicy foods, and so forth. Provide a menu planner/food intake documentation chart to the client or the caregiver.

37. Refer the client to a dietician to assess nutritional needs, diet, and cooking abilities.

38. Monitor and encourage the client's follow-through on the recommendations of professionals, such as the use of nutritional supplements, diet changes, sleep routine, and exercise.

39. Coordinate testing and follow-up treatment for sexually transmitted diseases or pregnancy. (See the Sexuality Concerns chapter in this Planner.)

40. Assist the client in negotiating the criminal justice system. (See the Legal Concerns chapter in this Planner.)

41. Assist the client in developing a list of relationships that have been affected by the client's severe and persistent mental illness symptoms.

42. Provide feedback to the client about how his/her behaviors or verbal messages have an impact on others, encouraging healthier relationship skills. (See the Social Skills chapter in this Planner.)

43. Facilitate family or conjoint therapy sessions to help the client and his/her significant others express emotions about relationship problems.

44. With the proper authorization to release information, inform the client's support system about his/her mental illness symptoms. Educate them about how they can assist the client or help him/her to access professional services.

45. Assist the client in identifying his/her history of recurrent mental illness symptoms, including periods of relative absence of symptoms. Utilize a timeline to identify these patterns.

46. Teach the client about his/her need for ongoing

care for a disease that is usually chronic in nature and that often misleads a patient into thinking that there is no need for treatment, medication, or therapy. Prompt the client to identify why this is a valid concern for him/her.

47. Directly confront the client's denial regarding his/her condition as a defense mechanism.

___. _____
   _____
   _____
___. _____
   _____
   _____
___. _____
   _____

DIAGNOSTIC SUGGESTIONS

Axis I:	295.70	Schizoaffective Disorder, Bipolar Type
	296.xx	Bipolar I Disorder
	296.89	Bipolar II Disorder
	301.13	Cyclothymic Disorder
	314.xx	Attention Deficit/Hyperactivity Disorder
	296.80	Bipolar Disorder NOS
	293.83	Mood Disorder Due to . . . [General Medical Condition]
	296.90	Mood Disorder NOS
	_____	_____
	_____	_____

MEDICATION MANAGEMENT

BEHAVIORAL DEFINITIONS

1. Failure to consistently take psychotropic medications as prescribed.
2. Verbalization of fears and dislike related to physical and/or emotional side effects of prescribed medications.
3. Failure to respond as expected to a prescribed medication regimen.
4. Lack of knowledge of medications as to their usefulness and potential side effects.
5. Statements of an unwillingness to take prescribed medications.
6. Alcohol or illicit drugs consumed along with psychotropic medications.
7. Medication interactions are causing negative side effects.

—. _____
   _____

—. _____
   _____

—. _____
   _____

LONG-TERM GOALS

1. Regular, consistent use of psychotropic medications at the prescribed dosage, frequency, and duration.
2. Increased understanding of the psychotropic medication dosage, the side effects, and the reasons for being prescribed.
3. Side effects reported on a timely basis and minimized in severity.
4. Decreased frequency and intensity of psychotic and other severe mental illness symptoms.

5. Support network of family, clinicians, and caregivers assist client in taking prescribed medication.
6. Decreased side effects of psychotropic medication through effective, timely regulation of dosage and type of medication.
7. Objectively measured blood levels indicate therapeutic dosage levels have been attained.

—. _____
   _____
   _____

—. _____
   _____
   _____

—. _____
   _____
   _____

SHORT-TERM OBJECTIVES

1. List all medications that are currently being prescribed and consumed. (1, 2, 3, 4)
2. Verbalize understood reasons for medications that are currently prescribed. (1, 5)
3. Verbalize accurate information regarding the reasons for, the side effects of, and the expected outcome of prescribed medications. (5, 6, 7, 8)
4. Identify the beliefs that are barriers to proper medication usage. (9, 10, 41)
5. Cooperate with a psychological evaluation to identify the cognitive barriers to proper medication usage. (11)
6. Identify the financial resources for payment for medication. (12, 13, 14, 15)

THERAPEUTIC INTERVENTIONS

1. Request that the client identify all currently prescribed medications, including names, times administered, and dosage.
2. Request that the client provide an honest, realistic description of his/her medication compliance.
3. Compare the client's description of medication usage with information from his/her medical chart or from his/her personal physician/psychiatrist.
4. Obtain blood level tests for medications expected to be present.
5. Request that the client identify the reason for the use of each medication; correct any misinformation.

7. Verbalize any thoughts of suicide. (16, 17, 18)

8. Cooperate with in-depth diagnostic procedures to accurately assess symptoms and medication effectiveness. (19, 20)

9. Take psychotropic medications as prescribed. (6, 7, 21, 22, 23)

10. Report the side effects and the effectiveness of the medications to the appropriate professional. (6, 22, 24, 25, 26)

11. Modify lifestyle to minimize the negative effects on medication effectiveness and side effects. (26)

12. Describe the expected positive effects of the medications. (22, 27)

13. Develop an increased ownership of the medication regimen. (28, 29)

14. Take the medications as administered by a caregiver or a family member. (23, 30, 31)

15. Take the medications responsibly on a single, day-to-day basis. (6, 30, 32, 34)

16. Take the medications responsibly on a week-to-week basis. (6, 30, 33, 34)

17. Take the medications responsibly on an ongoing, permanent basis. (6, 30, 35, 36)

18. Accept assistance from family members, peers, and others regarding the

6. Provide a written description to the client of his/her medications, the acceptable dosage levels, and the side effects.

7. Refer the client to a physician, a pharmacist, or other medical staff for additional information on specific medications.

8. Facilitate the involvement of a local pharmacist in the training about and the monitoring of medications.

9. Request that the client describe fears that he/she may experience regarding the use of the medication. Process these fears, correcting myths and misinformation.

10. Ask the client to identify the side effects that he/she is expecting or has experienced related to the medications; confer with the prescribing physician as to adjustments that are needed in the medication dosage and type.

11. Refer the client to a psychologist for intellectual testing relative to understanding the medication usage.

12. Assist the client in obtaining and maintaining employment. (See the Employment Problems chapter in this Planner.)

13. Refer the client to an appropriate agency to assist in obtaining entitlements (e.g., Medicaid, Social Security Disability).

medication usage.
(31, 37, 38, 39, 40)

19. Express social concerns that are related to the medication usage. (9, 41)

20. Attend a support group for the mentally ill. (42)

21. Obtain a more simplified administration of the medications. (43, 44)

22. Describe the extent of alcohol or illicit drug use. (45)

23. Terminate substance use or abuse. (46, 47)

24. Verbalize positive feelings about the improvement that is resulting from the medication's effectiveness. (42, 48, 49)

—. _____
   _____

—. _____
   _____

—. _____
   _____

14. Coordinate the client's access to free or low-cost medication programs through drug manufacturers or other resources.

15. Advocate for the client's use of generic drugs where appropriate.

16. Assess the client's suicidal ideation, taking into account the extent of ideation, the presence of a primary and a back-up plan, past attempts, and family history.

17. Remove the medication from the client's immediate access, if necessary.

18. Refer the client to crisis residential placement or to a psychiatric hospital when it is assessed that he/she may not be able to control suicidal intent.

19. Arrange for personality testing or other objective diagnostic evaluations to assist in diagnosis.

20. Arrange for psychiatric hospitalization to provide a structured, observational description and analysis of the client's diagnosis.

21. Arrange for a psychiatric evaluation to assess the need for new or additional psychiatric medications.

22. Monitor the client's use of and expected benefits of the medications.

23. Arrange for the client's medication to be adminis-

tered on a dose-by-dose basis, if necessary.

24. Review the side effects of the medication with the client and the medical staff.

25. Obtain a written release of information from the client to his/her primary physician or other health care providers to inform them of the medications and the expected side effects, risks, and benefits.

26. Arrange for the client to receive information about lifestyle habits (i.e., tobacco use, diet), that can be modified to decrease the side effects of the medication.

27. Educate the client about the expected or common psychiatric symptoms of his/her mental illness and how the medication is expected to ameliorate these symptoms.

28. Coordinate with the prescribing physician for the dosage to be within a certain range, when possible (e.g., 2 or 3 milligrams per day), to increase the client's authority over his own regimen.

29. Coordinate with the prescribing physician to allow the client to make minimal (i.e., biochemically nonsignificant) changes in the medication levels in consultation with a therapist, to increase the client's authority over and investment in the medication process.

30. Assess the client's ability to properly self-administer medications and arrange for supervision if necessary.

31. After obtaining the proper release of information from the client, request assistance from family members, roommates, peers, or caregivers to administer the medications to the client.

32. Arrange for daily medication drop-offs to the client, with instructions on which dosages to take at each time of day.

33. Arrange for prescriptions to be distributed in a multidose, compartmentalized daily medication box. Monitor the client for accurate usage of the pillbox.

34. Encourage the client to take his/her medications at a specific, consistent place and time every day.

35. Monitor the client's expected use of medications and accurate pill counts in pill bottles, on a sporadic basis.

36. Coordinate for all of the client's prescriptions (including nonpsychiatric medications) to be obtained from the same pharmacy.

37. Coordinate family or couples therapy to promote an understanding of the client's illness and the impact of that illness on the client's and the family's needs.

38. Train family members, peers, and others in the proper use and administration of medications, and to encourage or reinforce the client when he/she complies.

39. Request that family members, peers, and others provide information to the appropriate clinician about medication adherence, benefits, side effects, and prodromals.

40. Coordinate family members in providing the client with transportation to the clinic or pharmacy.

41. Request that the client identify social concerns that he/she may experience regarding medication usage (i.e., stigmatization, loss of independence); process these concerns to resolution.

42. Refer the client to a support group for individuals with severe and persistent mental illness.

43. Advocate with a physician for less complicated dosing times for the client's medications.

44. Investigate whether longer-acting or time-release medications (e.g., Depot medications) may be beneficial to the client.

45. Explore and assess the client's use of alcohol or illicit drugs.

46. Provide the client with information about the nega-

tive effects of substance abuse on his/her symptoms and the depotentiating effect of substances on his/her medications.

47. Refer the client for substance abuse treatment. (See the Chemical Dependence chapter in this Planner.)

48. Request that the client identify how the reduction in mental illness symptoms has improved his/her social or family system.

49. Coordinate the client obtaining individual therapy regarding adjustment to improved functioning relative to psychotic and other mental illness symptoms.

—. _____
    _____
    _____

—. _____
    _____
    _____

—. _____
    _____

DIAGNOSTIC SUGGESTIONS

Axis I:

297.1	Delusional Disorder
295.xx	Schizophrenia
295.10	Schizophrenia, Disorganized Type
295.30	Schizophrenia, Paranoid Type
295.90	Schizophrenia, Undifferentiated Type
295.60	Schizophrenia, Residual Type
295.70	Schizoaffective Disorder
296.xx	Bipolar I Disorder
296.89	Bipolar II Disorder
304.10	Sedative, Hypnotic, or Anxiolytic Dependence

305.40	Sedative, Hypnotic, or Anxiolytic Abuse
316	Mental Disorder Affecting a General Medical Condition
V15.81	Noncompliance With Treatment
_____	_____
_____	_____

PARANOIA

BEHAVIORAL DEFINITIONS

1. Fixed persecutory delusions regarding others, their intentions, and possible harm.
2. Extreme and consistent distrust of others without sufficient basis.
3. Expectations of being exploited or harmed by others.
4. Misinterpretation of benign events as having a threatening personal significance.
5. Auditory or visual hallucinations suggesting harm, threats to safety, or disloyalty.
6. Inclination to avoid others out of fear of being hurt or taken advantage of.
7. Easily offended, with angry, defensive responses.
8. Unwillingness to take advantage of treatment due to irrational persecutory beliefs (e.g., medication is poison, or the clinician is an enemy).
9. Potential for being violent as a defensive reaction to delusional or hallucinatory content of some person or agency being a threat to self or others.

__. _____
   _____
__. _____
   _____
__. _____
   _____

LONG-TERM GOALS

1. Reestablish and maintain reality-based orientation that is free from bizarre, suspicious thoughts or beliefs.
2. Show more trust in others by speaking positively of them and reporting comfort in socializing.
3. Develop realistic expectations of safety and risks that are related to interaction with others.
4. Learn coping skills to reduce effects of hallucinations or delusions.
5. Develop trustful relationships at work, at home, and in the community.
6. Reduce the level of vigilance around others.

—. _____
_____
_____
—. _____
_____
_____
—. _____
_____

SHORT-TERM OBJECTIVES

1. Describe the history, nature, and extent of paranoid ideation. (1, 2, 3, 4, 5)
2. Stabilize the current acute paranoid episode. (5, 6, 7, 8, 9)
3. Demonstrate a trusting relationship with a clinician by disclosing feelings and beliefs. (1, 2, 10, 11, 12)
4. Delineate specific paranoid beliefs. (10, 11, 13)
5. Verbalize an acceptance of the need for treatment. (14, 15)
6. Report a decrease in paranoid symptoms due to the

THERAPEUTIC INTERVENTIONS

1. Request that the client identify his/her history of persecutory hallucinations, delusions, or other paranoid symptoms.
2. Explore the nature and depth of the client's current feelings or ideas of paranoia.
3. Arrange for psychological testing to assess the extent and severity of paranoid symptoms.
4. Obtain information about the client's paranoid statements or behaviors from family members, police, guardian, or others who are familiar with the client.

regular use of psychiatric medications. (16, 17, 18, 19)

7. Report the side effects and effectiveness of the medications to the appropriate professional. (17, 18, 20)

8. Report a decrease in tardive dyskinesia symptoms. (20, 21, 22)

9. Family, friends, and caregivers respond calmly and firmly to the client's psychotic behaviors. (23, 24)

10. Report a decrease in the stress level as a contributing factor to paranoid ideation. (25, 26)

11. Cooperate with a physician's evaluation for medical or organic causes of paranoia. (27, 28, 29)

12. Comply with a neuropsychological assessment to rule out organic etiology as a basis for paranoid ideation. (29, 30)

13. Identify and remediate anxiety or obsessive-compulsive symptoms. (3, 26, 29, 31)

14. Describe the frequency and amount of alcohol or street drug use. (32)

15. Consent to treatment for substance abuse. (32, 33)

16. Report a perception of self and the world that is consistent with reality as perceived by most others. (34, 35, 36)

17. Describe self in a reality-based manner, accepting

5. Assess the client's immediate ability to maintain reality orientation and to not be a threat to the safety of himself/herself and others.

6. Provide the client with direct, basic instructions and with firm reassurances of his/her safety, confidentiality, and level of control.

7. Refer the client for immediate evaluation by a psychiatrist regarding psychotic symptoms and the need for psychiatric hospitalization.

8. Coordinate voluntary or involuntary psychiatric hospitalization if the client is so out of touch with reality as to pose a threat to himself/herself or others.

9. Arrange for the client to remain in a stable, supervised situation, including crisis adult foster care (AFC) placement or a friend/family member's home at least until the acute psychotic episode is stabilized.

10. Provide the client with empathic listening, displaying respect by accepting him/her, despite his/her angry or delusional presentation, but do not confirm the paranoid delusion.

11. Demonstrate a calm demeanor when the client discloses bizarre or antagonistic beliefs, to decrease his/her fear of rejection.

positive traits and denying special powers. (37, 38, 39)

18. Attend a support group for individuals with severe and persistent mental illness. (40)

19. Identify accurately the needs, feelings, and motivations of others. (40, 41)

20. Report an increased involvement in community-based social, recreational, volunteer, and/or vocational activities. (42, 43, 44)

21. Identify and accept minor faults in self. (37, 45)

22. Take antipsychotic medications consistently with or without supervision. (46)

23. Describe the recent perceived severe stressors that may have precipitated an acute psychotic break. (47)

24. Take steps to change the environment in a way that reduces the feelings of threat that are associated with it. (48)

25. Acknowledge that the belief about others being threatening is based more on subjective interpretation than on objective data. (49, 50, 51)

26. Decrease accusations of others' plans of harm toward self. (34, 41, 49, 52)

__. _____
    _____
__. _____
    _____

12. Reflect that the client's presentation, posture, and facial expression indicate intense emotion; show empathy for the client who is experiencing significant distress.

13. Ask the client open-ended questions about some of his/her delusions or paranoid beliefs. Refrain from arguing with the client about the validity of his/her beliefs.

14. Gently inform the client that his/her delusional persecutory beliefs are based in a mental illness, not in reality; educate the client about the symptoms of and the treatment for his/her mental illness.

15. Present the concept that some paranoid beliefs are due to a desire to avoid relationships that are perceived to be potentially harmful.

16. Refer the client to a physician or a psychiatrist for an evaluation of the need for psychiatric medication. Facilitate the prescription being filled.

17. Educate the client about the use and expected benefits of the medication. Take time to assure the client of the medication's level of safety.

18. Monitor the client's medication compliance and its effectiveness.

19. Arrange for direct, supervised administration of the medication, and the use of

—. _____

_____

liquid forms of medication to ensure regular adherence to the medication regimen.

20. Review the side effects of the medications with the client and the medical staff to identify possible tardive dyskinesia or other negative side effects.

21. Advocate with a physician/psychiatrist for an adjustment in the medications to reduce or to eliminate tardive dyskinesia.

22. Arrange for a regular assessment of the client's tardive symptoms, using the client, the staff, or a personal observation and/or an objective measurement scale [e.g., the *Abnormal Involuntary Movement Scale (AIMS)*].

23. Educate the client's family, friends, and caregivers about the symptoms of mental illness, emphasizing the nonvolitional aspects of the symptoms.

24. Utilize modeling and role playing to teach the family, friends, and caregivers how to give calm, assertive responses to paranoid behaviors, cautioning against challenges that are too vigorous for the client's delusional beliefs.

25. Teach or refer the client for training in skills for stress reduction, such as utilizing assertiveness, problem-solving, or stress-reducing

techniques. (See the Social Skills chapter in this Planner.)

26. Teach the client deep muscle relaxation and deep breathing techniques (e.g., see *The Relaxation and Stress Reduction Workbook, Fourth Edition,* by Davis, Eshelman, and McKay).

27. Refer the client for a complete physical evaluation to rule out or treat medical or organic causes for the client's paranoia.

28. Refer the client for an assessment of sensory loss (e.g., vision or hearing).

29. Coordinate the client's follow-up on evaluation concerns, such as prescriptions, lab work, or specialized assessments.

30. Refer the client for a neuropsychological assessment to rule out cognitive disorders such as dementia as the cause for paranoia.

31. Coordinate the treatments for anxiety or obsessive-compulsive disorder as concomitant factors in the client's paranoia. (See the Anxiety chapter in this Planner.)

32. Assess the client's nature and degree of substance use and the effect that this may have on his/her reality orientation and paranoia.

33. Refer or treat the client for substance abuse. (See the

Chemical Dependence chapter in this Planner.)

34. Encourage the client to develop and practice reality testing (e.g., ask the client to identify respected individuals with whom he/she can check the reality basis for delusional or paranoid thoughts).

35. Ask the client to record the specific delusions he/she has held. Review the journal material, helping the client identify the illogical nature of these beliefs.

36. Assist the client in identifying ways to investigate the validity of plausible (although unlikely) beliefs that he/she has; substantiate reality as the client tends to discount or misinterpret it.

37. Request that the client describe how he/she perceives himself/herself (e.g., identity, traits, abilities, etc.) and how to process perceptions with the clinician.

38. Reinforce the identification of positive, realistic self-attributions. Redirect the use of unsubstantiated negative self-perceptions or of an unrealistic view of powers or abilities (e.g., control over others, thought projecting, etc.).

39. Focus the client on identifying instances of positive regard from others.

40. Refer the client to a support group for individuals with severe and persistent mental illness.

41. Request that the client identify the needs, motivations, and feelings of others to increase the reality focus outside of himself/herself. Utilize role-playing, as well as role reversal, techniques to teach the client this other-oriented focus, and encourage a reality check of perceptions.

42. Coordinate the client's gradual involvement in community activities, volunteering, and other externally focused activities.

43. Encourage the client to increase his/her involvement in social relationships; reinforce the client's attempts in this area.

44. Attend social/recreational events with the client, allowing him/her to have control over the level of contact or support from the clinician during the outing. (See the Social Skill or the Recreation chapters in this Planner.)

45. Request that the client admit to one minor personality fault. Reinforce the ability to cope with negative feelings about oneself without feeling threatened.

46. Monitor the client for medication compliance and redi-

rect the client if he/she is noncompliant.

47. Probe for recent stressors that may have triggered the psychotic episode; explore the feelings surrounding the stressor that triggered the psychotic episode.

48. Assist the client in reducing threat in the environment (e.g., finding a safer place to live, arranging for regular visits from the caseworker, arranging for family members to call more frequently).

49. Provide alternative explanations for others' behaviors that counter the client's pattern of assumption of others' malicious intent.

50. Ask the client to complete a cost-benefit analysis (see *The Feeling Good Handbook* by Burns) around his/her specific fears; process this exercise with the therapist.

51. Conduct conjoint sessions to assess and reinforce verbalizations of trust toward significant others.

52. Confront irrational distrust of others and provide reality-based data to support trust.

__. _____
_____

__. _____
_____

__. _____
_____

DIAGNOSTIC SUGGESTIONS

Axis I:

295.30	Schizophrenia, Paranoid Type
295.70	Schizoaffective Disorder
296.xx	Bipolar I Disorder
296.89	Bipolar II Disorder
298.9	Psychotic Disorder NOS
300.01	Panic Disorder Without Agoraphobia
300.21	Panic Disorder With Agoraphobia
300.3	Obsessive-Compulsive Disorder
309.81	Posttraumatic Stress Disorder
_____	_____
_____	_____

Axis II:

301.0	Paranoid Personality Disorder
301.22	Schizotypal Personality Disorder
_____	_____
_____	_____

PARENTING

BEHAVIORAL DEFINITIONS

1. Severe and persistent mental illness symptoms affect interactions with the child.
2. Loss of custody of the child due to safety concerns or inability to care for the child.
3. Lack of interest in the child's activities.
4. Difficulty coping with the day-to-day stressors of parenting.
5. Disagreement with spouse or significant other regarding child-rearing practices.
6. Interference by the extended family due to concerns about the child's welfare.
7. The child takes advantage of the parent's ineffectiveness, which is related to severe and persistent mental illness symptoms.
8. The child experiences shame, embarrassment, or confusion due to the parent's mental illness symptoms.

__. _____

_____

__. _____

_____

__. _____

_____

LONG-TERM GOALS

1. Decrease the intensity, the frequency, and the duration of severe and persistent mental illness symptoms and their impact on parenting responsibilities.

2. Obtain the least restrictive, but safe and healthy, custody arrangement for the child.
3. Increase interest and involvement in the day-to-day activities of the child.
4. Develop the skills that are needed to cope with the natural stressors of parenting.
5. Negotiate an agreement with the spouse regarding the implementation of joint parenting strategies.
6. Develop a supportive connection with the extended family as an aid to parenting.
7. Child accepts and expresses his/her feelings about the parent's mental illness.

__. _____
_____
_____

__. _____
_____
_____

__. _____
_____

SHORT-TERM OBJECTIVES

1. Describe the history of parenting conflicts. (1, 2, 3)

2. Describe the current challenges and successes regarding parenting. (2, 4, 5, 6)

3. Verbalize an understanding of the connection between the mental illness symptoms and the struggles of parenting. (3, 7, 8, 9)

4. Cooperate with a physician evaluation for psychotropic medication. (10, 13)

5. Report a decrease in mental illness symptoms through the regular use of psycho-

THERAPEUTIC INTERVENTIONS

1. Explore the client's history of parenting concerns.

2. Develop a genogram or family tree to graphically display the various patterns and relationships within the family.

3. Develop a timeline of important events regarding parenting (e.g., births, relationships beginning or ending, loss or return of custody/visitation). Compare these events with milestones that are related to the illness (e.g., onset of symptoms, hospitalizations,

tropic medications.
(11, 12, 13)

6. Report the side effects and effectiveness of the medications to the appropriate professional. (11, 12, 14)

7. Attend classes that are focused on teaching effective parenting techniques. (13, 15)

8. Implement new skills for parenting. (15, 16, 17, 18)

9. Develop and implement a mutually agreeable plan for parenting with the partner. (13, 18, 19, 20)

10. Identify the impact of the mental illness symptoms on parenting interactions with the child. (21, 22)

11. Develop relief plans for stressful parenting situations or for periods of increased symptomology. (23, 24, 25)

12. Identify specific ways of displaying an increased interest in the child's needs and activities. (26, 27, 28)

13. Implement relaxation techniques and other stress relievers to decrease the normal strain of parenting and homemaking. (23, 29, 30, 31)

14. Attend a support group for individuals with severe and persistent mental illness. (32)

15. Child verbalizes an increased understanding of

etc.). Process with the client.

4. Ask the client (and his/her partner) to review current concerns regarding parenting, including the child's challenging behaviors, the approach taken with the child, and legal concerns (e.g., custody/visitation issues or Children's Protective Services involvement).

5. Remind the client (and his/her partner) to also focus on the successes and the positive traits of the child.

6. Refer the client for psychological testing to evaluate his/her ability to bond emotionally with the child with appropriate boundaries.

7. Educate the client (and his/her family/support system) about the symptoms of his/her mental illness by describing the specific disorder(s) and symptoms. Answer questions that the client and his/her family may have.

8. Refer the client and his/her family to books that provide information regarding the etiology, symptoms, and treatment of severe and persistent mental illness (e.g., *Schizophrenia: The Facts* by Tsuang and Faraone and *Bipolar Disorder: A Guide for Patients and Families* by Mondimore).

the parent's mental illness. (33, 34, 35)

16. Child expresses feelings about and accepts the parent's mental illness, without rejection of the parent. (33, 35, 36, 37)

17. Child attends an age-appropriate support group for family members of an individual with a severe mental illness. (38)

18. Child identifies accommodations that he/she can make that are due to the parent's mental illness. (39)

19. Child identifies healthy ways of reacting to peer teasing regarding the parent's mental illness. (40)

20. Identify decompensation signs, which indicate an inability to parent effectively. (41, 42)

21. Obtain the least restrictive custody and visitation arrangement while considering the child's safety and emotional needs. (2, 24, 41, 42, 43, 44)

22. Develop a working relationship with the estranged former partner/parent of the child. (45, 46)

23. Make and implement decisions regarding whether to voluntarily give up full or partial custody of the child. (41, 42, 47, 48, 49)

24. Make informed decisions about having children. (7, 8, 16, 50, 51)

9. Discuss the client's personal experience of severe and persistent mental illness symptoms and how these have affected his/her ability to parent effectively.

10. Arrange for an evaluation by a physician for a prescription for psychotropic medication.

11. Educate the client about the use and expected benefits of the medication.

12. Monitor the client's medication compliance and effectiveness.

13. Assist in obtaining day care for the client's children during his/her appointments for mental illness treatment.

14. Review the side effects of the medications with the client and the medical staff to identify possible side effects or the confounding influence of polypharmacy.

15. Refer the client to a parenting class.

16. Assign the client readings from books that provide guidance on effective parenting methods (e.g., *1-2-3 Magic: Effective Discipline for Children 2–12, Second Edition,* by Phelan, *Parenting Teens with Love and Logic: Preparing Adolescents for Responsible Adulthood* by Cline and Fay, or *Positive Parenting From A to Z* by Joslin).

__. _____
  _____
__. _____
  _____
__. _____
  _____

17. Use role playing, modeling, and behavioral rehearsal to help the client practice implementation of new parenting skills.

18. Assist the client in developing a list of priorities that he/she sees as most important to address when developing a parenting plan; develop parenting methods that are designed to meet those priorities.

19. Coordinate a conjoint session with the client's spouse/significant other to develop mutually acceptable plans for parenting of the child. Focus this meeting on the types of approaches to be used with the child.

20. Define intervals with the client at which to review the parenting plan that has been developed.

21. Explore with the client (and his/her significant other) those areas in which the client's mental illness symptoms may affect interactions with the child (e.g., transporting the child when manic, or meeting with the child's teacher when paranoia is not well controlled). Confront the client's denial of mental illness symptoms.

22. Assist the client (and his/her significant other) in developing contingency plans for areas in which the

client's mental illness symptoms may affect interactions with the child (e.g., the partner confiscates the car keys when he/she believes that the client is becoming manic).

23. Direct the client (and his/her significant other) to develop a listing of family members and other individuals who can provide short-term supervision to the client's child when the client is feeling overwhelmed by his/her parenting responsibilities.

24. Enlist the assistance of the extended family in providing long-term supervision and parenting to the child during acute phases of the client's mental illness.

25. Coordinate access to funds that are available for respite services to provide the client with short- or long-term periods of relief from the additional stress of parenting, or to spend time alone with one child.

26. Request that the client talk with the child to develop a list of three areas in which the client could take more interest in the child. Obtain a commitment from the client to log information daily about each area, sharing the observations with the child and the log with the clinician.

27. Suggest to the client that he/she set specific times to spend alone with each child. Encourage the client to treat this as a priority while still being flexible enough to reschedule if his/her mental illness symptoms are more acute.

28. Reinforce the client's increased involvement with the child. Prompt the client's support system to reinforce these behaviors as well.

29. Teach the client deep muscle relaxation and deep breathing techniques (e.g., see *The Relaxation and Stress Reduction Workbook, Fourth Edition,* by Davis, Eshelman, and McKay).

30. Help the client brainstorm diversionary activities (e.g., going for a walk, calling a friend, a hobby) that can relieve parenting stress.

31. Coordinate the client obtaining homemaking assistance to ease the burden of household tasks and to reduce his/her stress level.

32. Refer the client to a support group for individuals with a mental illness.

33. Coordinate individual and conjoint sessions for the child to ask questions that are related to the client's mental illness symptoms. Respond to the child's questions at an age-appropriate level.

34. Provide the child with age-appropriate written information about his/her parent's mental illness (e.g., *When Parents Have Problems: A Book for Teens and Older Children with an Abusive, Alcoholic, or Mentally Ill Parent* by Miller).

35. Coach the client about how to discuss his/her mental illness concerns in a manner in which the child can understand.

36. Explore with the child his/her feelings that are associated with the client's mental illness; explore those times when the symptoms have had a painful impact on the child's life.

37. Reinforce the need for the client to accept, without judgment, the feelings that the child experiences. Reassure the client that these feelings are not a personal attack.

38. Refer the child to either a multifamily support group or an age-appropriate support group for family members of an individual with a mental illness.

39. Assist the client and the child in identifying mild accommodations that can be made to increase functioning in the relationship (e.g., the adolescent will get ready for school on his/her own when the client's sleep pattern is erratic).

40. Brainstorm with the client's child about how to respond to teasing or other interference from peers that is relative to the parent's mental illness symptoms (e.g., ignoring teasing, report problems to an adult, etc.).

41. Enlist the client's assistance in developing a description of the level of decompensation at which he/she would see himself/herself as temporarily unable to function as a parent.

42. Assist the client in understanding the general guidelines under which the court or Child Protective Services unit will operate (whether he/she agrees or disagrees with these guidelines).

43. Assist the client in understanding and working through the multiple, intricate steps that occur during a custody or protective services case. Attend hearings as is necessary to provide emotional support to the client.

44. Refer the client to an attorney as is necessary.

45. Explore the degree of cooperative parenting that occurs with the client's former spouse; emphasize the need for this relationship to be a "working" relationship, focusing on the mutual job of raising the child. Friendship or other emotional needs should be sought elsewhere

if this confounds working together in the best interests of the children.

46. With a proper release of information, keep the estranged spouse informed of the client's general level of functioning, as it relates to his/her ability to care for the child.

47. Discourage the client from making any long-term, major life decisions during an acute phase of his/her illness.

48. Help the client identify the pros and cons of giving up custody. Be sure not to endorse one choice or another, but listen empathically as the client talks about issues in this area. Acknowledge the severe pain that making this decision may evoke.

49. Refer the client for grief counseling if he/she should decide to give up custody of the child.

50. Focus the client and his/her intimate partner onto the pros and cons of the choice to have children.

51. Refer the client and his/her intimate partner to a family planning clinic.

__. _____
   _____

__. _____
   _____

__. _____
   _____

DIAGNOSTIC SUGGESTIONS

Axis I:	297.1	Delusional Disorder
	295.xx	Schizophrenia
	295.10	Schizophrenia, Disorganized Type
	295.30	Schizophrenia, Paranoid Type
	295.90	Schizophrenia, Undifferentiated Type
	295.60	Schizophrenia, Residual Type
	295.70	Schizoaffective Disorder
	296.xx	Bipolar I Disorder
	296.89	Bipolar II Disorder
	V61.21	Physical Abuse or Neglect of a Child
	V61.20	Parent-Child Relational Problem
	_____	_____
	_____	_____

PSYCHOSIS

BEHAVIORAL DEFINITIONS

1. Bizarre content of thought (delusions of grandeur, persecution, reference, influence, control, somatic sensations, or infidelity).
2. Abnormal speech patterns as evidenced by tangential replies, incoherence, perseveration, and moving quickly from subject to subject.
3. Perceptual disturbance [hallucinations (including auditory, visual, tactile, or olfactory)].
4. Disorganized behavior, as evidenced by confusion, severe lack of goal direction, impulsiveness, or repetitive behaviors.
5. Paranoid thoughts and reactions, including extreme distrust, fear, and apprehension.
6. Psychomotor abnormalities such as a marked decrease in reactivity to environment; catatonic patterns such as stupor, rigidity, excitement, posturing, or negativism; unusual mannerisms or grimacing.
7. Extreme agitation, including a high degree of irritability, anger, unpredictability, or impulsive physical acting out.
8. Bizarre dress or grooming.
9. Disturbed affect (blunted, none, flattened, or inappropriate).
10. Relationship withdrawal (withdrawal from involvement with the external world and preoccupation with egocentric ideas and fantasies, feelings of alienation).

__. _____
   _____
   _____
__. _____
   _____
   _____
__. _____
   _____

LONG-TERM GOALS

1. Control or eliminate active psychotic symptoms so that supervised functioning is positive and medication is taken consistently.
2. Increase goal-directed behaviors.
3. Focus thoughts on reality.
4. Normalize speech patterns, which can be evidenced by coherent statements, attentions to social cues, and remaining on task.
5. Interact with others without defensiveness or anger.

___. _____

_____

_____

___. _____

_____

___. _____

_____

SHORT-TERM OBJECTIVES

1. Describe the history and the current status of psychotic symptoms. (1, 2, 3, 4)
2. Stabilize the current acute psychotic episode. (5, 6, 7, 8)
3. Monitor physical needs that are related to the psychotic episode. (9, 10, 11)
4. Decrease the suicide risk or the potential thereof. (6, 12, 13)
5. Modify the environment to decrease the stimuli and the effects of psychotic confusion. (14, 15, 16, 17)
6. Obtain immediate, temporary support or supervision from friends, peers, or family members. (7, 18, 19, 20)

THERAPEUTIC INTERVENTIONS

1. Request that the client identify his/her history of hallucinations, delusions, or other psychotic symptoms.
2. Ask the client about his/her current psychotic symptoms.
3. Coordinate psychological testing to assess the extent and the severity of the client's psychotic symptoms.
4. Request that a family member provide information about the client's history of psychotic behaviors.
5. Refer the client for an immediate evaluation by a psychiatrist regarding his/her psychotic symptoms and a possible prescription for antipsychotic medication.

7. Reorient self to place and time. (21, 22, 23, 24)

8. Report a decrease in psychotic symptoms through the consistent use of psychotropic medications. (5, 25, 26, 27)

9. Report the side effects and the effectiveness of the medications to the appropriate professional. (26, 27, 28, 29)

10. Family, friends, and caregivers demonstrate techniques to cope with the client's psychotic behaviors. (19, 30, 31)

11. Identify the environmental triggers or the precipitating events that are related to increased psychotic symptoms. (1, 32, 33)

12. Identify and understand the role of internal triggers (e.g., internal emotional states), which precipitate a decompensation. (1, 32, 34)

13. Identify the role of stress in decompensation, as well as internal and external indicators of stress. (34, 35, 36)

14. Implement healthy responses to stressful situations. (35, 36, 37, 38)

15. Identify the early warning signs of symptom exacerbation and decompensation. (30, 39, 40)

16. Decrease substance abuse as a precipitating trigger. (41, 42)

6. Coordinate voluntary or involuntary psychiatric hospitalization if the client is a threat to himself/herself or others and/or is unable to provide for his/her own basic needs.

7. Arrange for the client to remain in a stable, supervised situation [e.g., crisis adult foster care (AFC) placement or a friend's/family member's home].

8. Coordinate mobile crisis response services (e.g., physical exam, psychiatric evaluation, medication access, triage to impatient care, etc.) in the client's home environment (including jail, personal residence, homeless shelter, or street setting).

9. Obtain vital signs such as blood pressure, heart rate, and pulse. Refer to medical personnel for immediate treatment if needed.

10. Inquire about food intake and nutrition. With permission, check the client's food resources (e.g., look in the cabinets and the refrigerator to assure that adequate food is available).

11. Ask the client about his/her sleep pattern and the need for possible sleep aids. Ask caregivers about the client's and their own recent sleep patterns.

17. Coordinate an early link from a more restrictive into a less restrictive setting. (24, 43)

18. Caregivers, friends, and family members report reduced stress regarding the client's behavior. (30, 31, 44)

19. Implement cognitive techniques to increase resistance to subsequent psychotic episodes. (45, 46, 47, 48)

20. Verbalize the acceptance of mental illness and the decreased feelings of stigmatization. (30, 47, 49, 50, 51)

21. Attend a support group for others with severe mental illness. (51)

__. _____
   _____

__. _____
   _____

__. _____
   _____

12. Perform a suicide assessment and take all necessary precautionary steps, if necessary.

13. Remove potentially hazardous materials, such as firearms or excess medication, if indicated.

14. Provide a quiet, dimly lit environment.

15. Approach an acutely psychotic client in a calm, confident, open, direct, yet soothing manner (e.g., approach slowly, face toward the client with open body language, speak slowly and clearly).

16. Utilize caregivers with whom the client is familiar as much as possible to avoid anxiety in the client regarding interacting with strangers.

17. Maintain a regular schedule of activities for the client to establish a routine that is predictable.

18. Develop a crisis plan to provide supervision and support to the client on an intensive basis.

19. Train support persons to provide direct, nonreactive, calm responses to the client's psychotic behaviors.

20. Coordinate access to round-the-clock, professional consultation (e.g., a 24-hour professionally staffed crisis line) to caregivers and the client.

21. Provide both visual and verbal cues to focus on reality (e.g., write the date, time, and place in a clearly visible area).

22. Place a wristband on the client's arm with the date, place, and name.

23. Focus on real events in basic, concrete terms.

24. Reinforce the appropriate focus on reality, gradually returning the client to a less restrictive environment and decreased supervision.

25. Consult with the treating physician regarding sleep-inducing medications to provide the client and the caregivers time to regroup, relative to the current psychotic episode.

26. Educate the client about the use and expected benefits of psychotropic medications.

27. Monitor the client's medication compliance and effectiveness.

28. Review the side effects of the medications with both the client and the medical staff to identify the possible confounding influence of polypharmacy.

29. Monitor the client for side effects of long-term use of neuroleptic medications (e.g., tardive dyskinesia, muscle rigidity, dystonia).

30. Educate the client's family, friends, and caregivers about the symptoms of

mental illness, emphasizing
the nonvolitional aspects of
the symptoms.

31. Role-play calm, assertive responses to psychotic behaviors with the client's family,
friends, and caregivers.
Focus on providing the
client with specific, short directions rather than arguing about reality.

32. Request that the client
identify specific behaviors,
situations, and feelings that
occurred prior to decompensation or psychotic episodes.

33. Help the client identify specific environmental trigger
patterns for acute psychotic
episodes based on his/her
history.

34. Identify the client's specific
emotional conflicts, which increase his/her vulnerability
to psychotic decompensation.

35. Request that the client
identify three emotional indicators of stress (e.g., anx-
iousness, uncertainty,
anger) and how they affect
his/her functioning.

36. Request that the client identify three physical indicators
of stress (e.g., tense muscles,
headaches, psychomotor agitation) and how they affect
his/her functioning.

37. Teach the client assertiveness and other adaptive
communication techniques.

38. Refer to an activity therapist
for stress reduction activi-

ties (e.g., exercise programs, hobbies, or social clubs).

39. Request that the client identify symptoms that indicate that he/she is decompensating.

40. Train the family, friends, and caregivers about the client's list of decompensation indicators, so they can take appropriate action to get professional services for the client.

41. Encourage the client to decrease or to discontinue substance use, including drugs, alcohol, nicotine, and caffeine. (See the Chemical Dependence chapter of this Planner.)

42. Refer the client to a substance abuse treatment program.

43. Meet with the client early in the stay at the hospital or other more restrictive setting to coordinate his/her release and return to a less restrictive setting.

44. Teach problem-solving, respite care, and assertiveness skills to assist caregivers in meeting their own needs when they feel overly stressed by the client's psychosis.

45. Provide or refer the client for cognitive behavioral therapy that is focused on challenging the underpinning beliefs of the delusions, and that can assist

the client in adjusting to the reality of his/her illness.

46. Teach the client distraction techniques (e.g., listening to a personal stereo, reading out loud) to move his/her focus away from the hallucinations.

47. Desensitize the client's fear of his/her hallucinations by allowing or encouraging him/her to talk about them, their frequency, their intensity, and their meaning.

48. Encourage the client to seek frequent reality testing to challenge his/her distorted beliefs (e.g., compare his/her cognitions with the experience of trusted caregivers, friends, and family).

49. Encourage the client to express his/her feelings, related to acceptance of the mental illness.

50. Explain the nature of the psychotic process, its biochemical component, and its confusing effect on rational thought.

51. Refer the client to a support group for individuals with a mental illness.

___. _____

_____

___. _____

_____

___. _____

_____

DIAGNOSTIC SUGGESTIONS

Axis I:	297.1	Delusional Disorder
	295.xx	Schizophrenia
	295.10	Schizophrenia, Disorganized Type
	295.20	Schizophrenia, Catatonic Type
	295.90	Schizophrenia, Undifferentiated Type
	295.30	Schizophrenia, Paranoid Type
	295.70	Schizoaffective Disorder
	296.xx	Bipolar I Disorder
	296.89	Bipolar II Disorder
	293.xx	Psychotic Disorder Due to . . . [General Medical Condition]
	298.9	Psychotic Disorder NOS

RECREATION

BEHAVIORAL DEFINITIONS

1. Lack of involvement in recreational activities.
2. Lack of interest in leisure activities.
3. Limited knowledge of recreational opportunities due to inexperience.
4. Embarrassment, frustration, or agitation act as a barrier to involvement in recreational activities.
5. Mental illness symptoms disrupt involvement in recreational opportunities.
6. Discrimination due to mental illness symptoms prohibits involvement in community activities.
7. Medication has a negative influence on coordination or other skills that are necessary for some recreational activities (e.g., sports).
8. Lack of invitations to recreational activities due to limited social contacts.
9. Inability to pay for or obtain transportation to recreational activities.

__. _____
   _____
__. _____
   _____
   _____
__. _____
   _____

LONG-TERM GOALS

1. Increase involvement in recreational activities.
2. Learn about general recreational opportunities.

3. Gain proficiency in the skills that are necessary for involvement in chosen recreational areas.
4. Decrease the effects of severe and persistent mental illness symptoms on recreational activities.
5. Increase assertiveness about the right to be involved in desired recreational areas.
6. Limit side effects of medications, increasing the ability to be involved in physical activities.
7. Develop social contacts with whom to share recreational activities.
8. Obtain funds, transportation, or other prerequisites for recreational activities.

—. _____
_____
—. _____
_____
—. _____

SHORT-TERM OBJECTIVES

1. Describe the history of recreational involvement. (1, 2, 3)
2. Identify the scope and nature of the effects of the mental illness symptoms on recreational pursuits. (3, 4, 5, 6, 7)
3. Cooperate with a referral to a physician for a psychotropic medication evaluation. (8)
4. Report a decrease in the effects of the mental illness symptoms through the regular use of psychotropic medications. (8, 9, 10)

THERAPEUTIC INTERVENTIONS

1. Request that the client describe his/her history of participation in recreational activities.
2. Ask the client about recreational activities that he/she has utilized in the past, but that are not currently utilized or available.
3. Develop a graphic display, such as a timeline, to show the history of the client's recreational involvement, as well as milestones that are related to severe and persistent mental illness (i.e., onset of symptoms, hospitalizations, or beginning of treatment).

5. Report the side effects and effectiveness of the medications to the appropriate professional. (9, 10, 11, 12)

6. Identify past and current preferences for leisure activities. (13, 14)

7. Sample a wide range of leisure activities by participating in a variety of recreational activities. (14, 15, 16)

8. Identify preferences for new recreational activities that have been explored. (13, 17, 18)

9. Identify the emotional barriers to increased involvement in leisure activities. (19, 20)

10. List social/recreational activities that are available within the community. (21, 22)

11. Obtain financial resources for recreational activities. (23, 24, 25)

12. Increase access to remote recreational activities through the use of transportation that is provided by others. (26, 27)

13. Demonstrate new skills that are useful for participation in recreational activities. (7, 14, 28, 29, 30)

14. Attend a support group for individuals with severe and persistent mental illness. (31)

15. Implement newly learned social skills that are neces-

4. Educate the client on the symptoms of his/her mental illness, through informal question-and-answer sessions, or through referral to texts such as *Schizophrenia: The Facts* by Tsuang and Faraone or *Bipolar Disorder: A Guide for Patients and Families* by Mondimore.

5. Request that the client identify two situations in which his/her mental illness symptoms have affected his/her involvement in recreational activities.

6. Help the client make the connection between mental illness symptoms and social/ recreational problems (e.g., paranoia prohibits involvement in group activities, or mania confuses or puts others off).

7. Help the client identify the recreation areas in which he/she has had little experience due to severe and persistent mental illness symptoms.

8. Refer the client for an evaluation by a physician regarding the need for psychotropic medications.

9. Educate the client about the use and the expected benefits of the medication.

10. Monitor the client's medication compliance and effectiveness.

11. Review the side effects of the medications with the

sary for recreational involvement with others. (31, 32, 33, 34)

16. Caregivers use incidental learning techniques to teach the client social skills. (35, 36)

17. Initiate recreational activities during free time. (14, 37, 38, 39)

18. Report feeling more comfortable in new social or recreational activities. (39, 40, 41)

19. Increase the frequency of engagement in activities involving physical exercise and fitness. (14, 38, 42, 43)

20. Increase involvement in social relationships. (31, 32, 34, 44, 45)

21. Utilize relaxation techniques to manage stress while engaged in social/ recreational activities. (33, 40, 46)

22. Gain freedom from other responsibilities to enjoy recreational activities. (47, 48)

23. List the supportive resources that can be called on if abuse or discrimination occurs as social horizons expand. (32, 49)

24. Develop recreational habits that are not associated with substance use or abuse. (31, 50)

client and the medical staff to identify the possible confounding influence of polypharmacy.

12. Acknowledge the manner in which the side effects of the medications may inhibit the client's involvement in some recreational activities (e.g., slowed reaction time decreases motor dexterity); confer with the prescribing physician regarding a possible change in the client's medication regimen.

13. Request that the client identify at least two recreational activities that he/she has enjoyed in the past.

14. Refer the client to an activity or recreational therapist for an assessment of his/her current interests and abilities that are relative to leisure interests.

15. Contract with the client to pursue a short-term involvement with a variety of activities. Emphasize the need to explore several different areas to develop interests.

16. Develop a schedule of activities that samples a broad range of types of activities, settings, length of time, level of involvement, cultural needs and social contact.

17. Review the sampling of activities on a regular basis.

18. Request that the client identify his/her preferences

—. _____

_____

—. _____

_____

—. _____

_____

from the activities that he/she has experienced.

19. Explore the client's reactions to difficult social experiences in the past. Help the client to identify specific emotions.

20. Acknowledge the emotions that may be limiting the client's willingness to be involved in new activities, including fear, embarrassment, or uncertainty.

21. Request that the client develop an inventory of activities that are available in the community. Request that he/she review information from the local newspaper, telephone book, or magazines.

22. Obtain additional resources for the client to review regarding the recreational activities that are available in the community (e.g., brochures from a local tourism board, current events calenders, etc.).

23. Assist the client in developing a regular source of income. (See the Financial Needs and the Employment Problems chapters in this Planner.)

24. Facilitate the client's access to funds from the agency or from community organizations for assisting people with disabilities.

25. Contact recreational businesses in the community for sponsorship of the client's

involvement in recreational
activities (e.g., free tickets
or supplies).

26. Coordinate ride sharing
    with other clients or commu-
    nity members who are at-
    tending recreational events.

27. Assist the client in iden-
    tifying and scheduling
    community-based trans-
    portation resources for
    his/her use in recreational
    activities.

28. Provide a leisure educator
    or a recreational therapist
    to teach the client the basic
    technical skills for partici-
    pating in leisure activities.

29. Provide the client with ac-
    cess to on-line services as a
    way to have increased social
    contact in a safer setting.

30. Incorporate cooking and
    meal preparation as a por-
    tion of the recreational
    skills training as an added
    incentive for the completion
    of each training session.

31. Refer the client to a support
    group for people with severe
    and persistent mental ill-
    ness.

32. Model social skills to the
    client (e.g., assertiveness,
    clear communication, han-
    dling anger). Review/critique
    the client's use of these skills.

33. Refer the client to individ-
    ual therapy to help him/her
    learn social skills.

34. Utilize role-playing, behav-
    ioral rehearsal, and role re-

versal techniques to help the client understand the use of social skills.

35. Train the caregivers/staff in the use of incidental learning techniques (e.g., teaching the client social and recreational skills during the course of everyday activities).

36. Monitor the ongoing use of incidental learning techniques and provide feedback to the staff/caregivers.

37. Provide the client with a listing of recreational activities in which he/she has indicated some interest. Urge the client to utilize this listing to initiate activity during free times.

38. Provide the client and the caretakers with a chart to monitor and track the involvement that the client has had in various activities.

39. Verbally reinforce the client's involvement in recreational activities. Request that the client identify the positive effects of this increased involvement.

40. Attend recreational activities with the client to provide encouragement and support. Allow the client to be in charge of the level of involvement that the clinician maintains.

41. Solicit volunteers from the client's family and peers to

attend recreational activities with him/her.

42. Refer the client to a physician for a complete physical examination to determine the client's ability to participate in physical activities.

43. Coordinate the client's physical exercise involvement with others who have similar interests, including the nondisabled population, as well as others with severe and persistent mental illness.

44. With the proper release of information, provide information to nondisabled peers about how to best cope with their friend's severe and persistent mental illness symptoms.

45. Review periodically with the client the successes and difficulties that he/she has experienced in social settings.

46. Teach the client relaxation techniques to be used in social situations to reduce stress (e.g., see *The Relaxation and Stress Reduction Workbook, Fourth Edition,* by Davis, Eshelman, and McKay).

47. Coordinate the provision of respite services to the client who has responsibility for children or other dependent individuals.

48. Incorporate a recreational component into the client's day programming or sup-

ported employment program.

49. Review the possible situations in which an individual with severe and persistent mental illness might be manipulated or abused. Remind the client of the support system that he/she has and should use if he/she is uncertain about treatment from others.

50. Emphasize to the client the need for developing social and recreational activities that are not related to the use of mood-altering substances.

__. _____

_____

__. _____

_____

__. _____

_____

DIAGNOSTIC SUGGESTIONS

Axis I:	297.1	Delusional Disorder
	295.xx	Schizophrenia
	295.10	Schizophrenia, Disorganized Type
	295.30	Schizophrenia, Paranoid Type
	295.90	Schizophrenia, Undifferentiated Type
	295.60	Schizophrenia, Residual Type
	295.70	Schizoaffective Disorder
	296.3x	Major Depressive Disorder, Recurrent
	296.xx	Bipolar I Disorder
	296.89	Bipolar II Disorder
	300.23	Social Phobia
	303.90	Alcohol Dependence

	304.30	Cannabis Dependence
	304.90	Other (or Unknown) Substance Dependence
	_____	_____
	_____	_____
Axis II:	301.0	Paranoid Personality Disorder
	301.22	Schizotypal Personality Disorder
	301.83	Borderline Personality Disorder
	301.82	Avoidant Personality Disorder
	_____	_____
	_____	_____

SELF-DETERMINATION

BEHAVIORAL DEFINITIONS

1. Lack of choice in daily life, school, residence, or vocation.
2. Limited experience with making decisions.
3. Poor planning for the near and the distant future, which results in difficult transitions.
4. Decreased responsibilities and opportunities due to mental impairments.
5. Agencies have been dictating the options/services that are available, limiting the freedom of choice.
6. Lack of skills necessary for living independently.
7. Vocational and/or residential placement failures due to a lack of appropriate decision-making skills and an inability to adjust to changing situations.
8. Lack of assertiveness, decision making, and problem solving resulting from caregivers overprotecting the client.
9. Treatment agency structure sets up barriers to the client's choice of services and providers.
10. Client, family, caregivers, and clinicians lack the knowledge or the training in the concepts of self-determination.

—. _____
_____

—. _____
_____

—. _____
_____

LONG-TERM GOALS

1. Maximize available choices in all aspects of life.
2. Advocate assertively for own needs and preferences.
3. Increase understanding and identification of own needs and preferences.
4. Increase belief in self-worth and in ability to pursue own needs and desires.
5. Develop planning and goal-setting skills.
6. Caregivers consistently encourage and reinforce all of the client's movement toward his/her own decision making.
7. Develop and maintain lasting relationships with handicapped and nonhandicapped peers.
8. Plan for future needs to prepare for life-span transition periods.
9. Gain access to integrated employment, social, and community opportunities.
10. Treatment agency revises structure to enhance the client's attempts to become more independent.
11. Caregivers, client, family, and clinicians display a clear understanding of the intent and mechanics of self-determination.

—. _____

_____

—. _____

_____

—. _____

_____

SHORT-TERM OBJECTIVES	THERAPEUTIC INTERVENTIONS
1. Verbalize an understanding of the process of person-centered planning or self-determination. (1, 2)	1. Assess the client's understanding of self-determination or person-centered planning ideas.
2. Clinician, caregivers, and family verbalize an understanding of the process and spirit of person-centered planning and self-determination. (2, 3, 4)	2. Help the client and caregivers identify examples of self-determination in their own lives as well as others'. Give personal examples of

3. Participate in an assessment of the skills that will facilitate self-determination. (5, 6)

4. Develop a plan for a person-centered planning meeting. (7, 8, 9, 10, 11)

5. Prepare for the person-centered planning meeting by clarifying own goals and barriers to those goals. (12, 13, 14, 15)

6. Participate in a person-centered planning meeting. (16, 17, 18)

7. Identify short- and long-term hopes, dreams, and desires. (19, 20)

8. Increase involvement in chosen recreational, social, employment, financial, and residential activities. (21, 22)

9. Demonstrate the ability to make choices that are safe, responsible, informed, and not harmful to self or others. (21, 23, 24, 25)

10. Choose service providers based on own preferences, needs, and financial resources. (26, 27, 28)

11. Service providers verbalize a recognition that the client has a choice of providers and must be given respectful, service-oriented treatment. (3, 29)

12. Advocate for self, representing own best interest and exercising choices. (30, 31, 32)

how the clinician experiences self-determination. Provide factual information to the client as needed.

3. Invite the client and his/her family and caregivers to agency trainings on person-centered planning and self-determination.

4. Encourage the client and his/her family and caregivers to discuss the use of self-determination principles relative to the client's treatment, dreams, and desires.

5. Assess the client's strengths and weaknesses in self-determination (e.g., autonomy, self-regulation, psychological empowerment, self-realization). Use the results to promote the client's involvement in planning future goals with the support of his/her family.

6. Share the findings from the client's self-determination assessment, emphasizing his/her strengths.

7. Facilitate the client developing an agenda for a person-centered planning meeting (i.e., what goals the client would like to achieve); provide the client with some examples of possible goals, but pursue his/her input.

8. Assist the client in inviting all of the individuals whom he/she would like to be present during the person-

13. Implement problem-solving techniques to resolve daily-life issues. (33, 34)

14. Express preferences and choices in all aspects of personal life. (31, 35, 36, 37, 38)

15. Review own behavior and assess whether it is focused on goal attainment. (39, 40)

16. Develop cooperative relationships with peers, both with and without mental illness. (41, 42, 43, 44)

17. Increase participation in community-based opportunities for social, recreation, and vocational activities. (45, 46, 47)

18. Family members support and reinforce the client in making his/her own decisions. (48, 49, 50)

19. Client and family advocate for greater self-determination within the agency and the mental health/welfare system. (51, 52)

—. _____
_____

—. _____
_____

—. _____
_____

centered planning meeting (e.g., clinicians, family members, peers, advocates, friends, etc). Allow the client to choose the members, as well as how they are invited and where the meeting is held.

9. Review with the client the people whom he/she would prefer not to have at his/her meeting, and the procedure that he/she wishes to use if that person indicates an interest in coming. Review the implications of not inviting a specific individual.

10. Request the client to choose a facilitator for his/her person-centered planning meeting. Emphasize that this does not have to be a clinical person.

11. Allow the client to identify "off-limits" topics (e.g., topics that he/she does not wish to be brought up at the person-centered planning meeting). Prompt the client to identify a setting in which he/she would be willing to discuss those topics.

12. Taking direction from the client, use a written personal planning workbook such as _PATH: A Workbook for Planning Positive Possible Futures_ by Pearpoint to review the client's dreams and desires for his/her life.

13. Assist the client in articulating his/her current daily

life, relationships, personal history, preferences, dreams, hopes and fears, community choices, and issues that are related to home, career, and health.

14. Request that the client identify barriers that interfere with his/her stated desires; assist the client in identifying the kinds of support that are needed to attain future goals and dreams.

15. Request that the client identify areas in which he/she would like to improve (e.g., living situation, work setting, relationships).

16. Facilitator or client call the person-centered planning meeting to order, focusing the participants on the client and his/her desires and needs.

17. Ask the participants in the person-centered planning meeting to direct their comments to the client, rather than the clinician or the facilitator.

18. Ask the client to answer first, then the rest of the participants, in posing questions such as "Who is _____?", "What are _____'s strengths and problems?", "What supports, accommodations, or barriers exist?", and/or "What shall we put in the action plan for goals/objectives?"

19. Assist the client in making a list of his/her short- and long-term goals. Request

that the client identify his/her favorite three. Ensure that continuity exists between short-term and long-term goals and that those goals are objectively observable and obtainable in a reasonable amount of time.

20. Assist the client in identifying and creating conditions that will facilitate the realization of his/her goals and desires (e.g., expand and deepen friendships, increase community participation, exercise more control and choice in life, and develop competencies). Identify creative solutions for breaking the existing barriers to identified goals.

21. Explore the client's desires to participate in a wide range of possible activities (e.g., social contacts, independent living, volunteer or work placement, service groups, church, or recreational events) that promote community integration and the development of self-determination skills.

22. Arrange for all significant people in the client's life (e.g., family, advocates, community members, staff, and agency personnel) to brainstorm creative options for expansion of the client's personal choices and to commit to assisting the

client in attaining the identified goals.

23. Assess the client's potential
for making adverse choices.
Help determine the risk of
the choices that result in
physical and/or mental
harm by talking with the
client and his/her family
and professionals, as well as
direct observation.

24. Weigh the assessed risk-of-
harm level against the
client's right to make
his/her own choices. Factor
in the likelihood of short- or
long-term harm, physical or
psychological harm, direct
or indirect harm, and predictable or unpredictable
harm to himself/herself or
others. Use these findings
to determine the degree of
freedom of choice that is
best suited for the client
(e.g., total independence
with unrestricted choice or
limited independence with
restricted options available
from which to choose).

25. Obtain a consensus from
the client and his/her family
and support staff regarding
the level of risk that is tol-
erable and the degree of
freedom of choice that is
his/her right.

26. Remind the client (or
guardian) that he/she has a
choice about the services
provided, who provides
them, and where he/she receives these services.

27. Develop a listing or a network of providers for the client (or guardian) to choose from, which may include the clinician's own services.

28. List the costs of all the services that are currently provided. Provide the client with the cost of each individual service/provider who is available and appropriate for meeting his/her needs. Allow the client (or guardian) to choose whatever services and providers that they see fit within their financial resources.

29. Focus the service providers on the need to provide customer service, and emphasize that the client has a choice of providers available (help the provider adopt a "We need them!" philosophy, rather than "They need us.").

30. Help the client identify actual examples from his/her life when he/she has used decision-making skills such as gathering information, weighing pros and cons, consulting with others, and so forth.

31. Teach the client techniques for assertive self-advocacy, such as those listed in *The Self-Advocacy Manual for Consumers* by the Michigan Protection and Advocacy Service, Inc., or *The Self-Advocacy Workbook* by

Gardner. Promote self-advocacy and leadership by providing practice opportunities whenever possible (e.g., with counselors, personal care support personnel, and residential supervisors).

32. Teach the client the difference between passive, assertive, and aggressive behaviors. Model assertive, aggressive, and passive responses to the same situation, and request that the client identify the most effective style.

33. Teach the client problem-solving techniques, such as those in *Thinking It Through: Teaching a Problem-Solving Strategy for Community Living* by Foxx and Bittle. Use role playing and modeling to reinforce these techniques.

34. Encourage the client to keep a problem-solving log of his/her conflicts to prompt regular use of problem-solving techniques. Review the problem-solving logs with the client.

35. Assess the client's responses to various activities and situations to better understand his/her preferences (e.g., approach, verbalizations, gestures, and affect).

36. Provide opportunities for the client to choose in all areas of his/her life (e.g.,

leisure, shopping, mealtime, lifestyle, or employment).

37. Stress with the family, the caregivers, and the support staff the importance of the client being able to express his/her own choices and preferences and to have them honored.

38. Provide many learning opportunities and plan for self-determination skill generalization by expanding the range of situations to which the client responds, and by providing similarity between learning stimuli and the client's natural environment.

39. Review with the client his/her decisions, and encourage him/her to evaluate his/her own behavior to determine if it is compatible with the identified goals. Assist the client in changing his/her behavior to obtain goals as needed.

40. Discuss with the client the reinforcers that he/she desires, and that they can be established by him/her as independently attainable, contingent on the occurrence of his/her own predetermined target behaviors.

41. Teach the client social skills through didactic presentation and role playing (e.g., basic conversational skills, self-assertion, honesty, truthfulness, and how to handle teasing). (See the

Social Skills chapter in this Planner.)

42. Arrange for the client to utilize social skills in situations that he/she has identified as desirable.

43. Urge and reinforce the client for taking risks in participating in social situations with people who have disabilities and with those who do not.

44. With proper authorization to release information, provide feedback to the family and (non–mentally ill) peers about how best to approach the client and his/her needs (e.g., equality, respect, reciprocity of friendship).

45. Teach the client about the availability and the use of community resources. (See the Independent Activities of Daily Living (IADL) chapter in this Planner.)

46. Teach the client community access skills. (See the Independent Activities of Daily Living (IADL) in this Planner).

47. Assist the client in obtaining employment, via a supported employment referral, or assisting with the preparation of a resume, job applications, and so forth. (See the Employment Problems chapter in this Planner.)

48. Encourage the family and the caregivers to identify a plan of supporting lifelong

learning opportunities and experiences for the client. Assist in identifying the specific steps to promote the client's decision making, problem solving, and goal setting and attainment, as well as his/her self-awareness and knowledge in the home.

49. Demonstrate to the family the many opportunities throughout the day that the client can use for exerting choices and preferences (e.g., meal choices, schedule for the day, clothing choices). Encourage the family to foster independence by helping only when needed, permitting the client to maximize his/her abilities.

50. Emphasize with the family that the freedom to make choices, even harmful ones, is a freedom that most people value. Encourage the family to allow the client to assume responsibility for his/her own actions and the natural consequences, both positive and negative, that result.

51. Encourage the family and the client to be involved in positions of leadership, advocacy, or advising within the agency.

52. Support and encourage the family's efforts in petitions, lobbying, writing letters to legislators, and/or meeting

with legislators to advocate
for the right of the mentally
ill to self-determination.

—. _____

_____

—. _____

_____

—. _____

_____

DIAGNOSTIC SUGGESTIONS

Axis I:
297.1	Delusional Disorder
295.xx	Schizophrenia
295.10	Schizophrenia, Disorganized Type
295.20	Schizophrenia, Catatonic Type
295.90	Schizophrenia, Undifferentiated Type
295.30	Schizophrenia, Paranoid Type
295.70	Schizoaffective Disorder
296.xx	Bipolar I Disorder
296.89	Bipolar II Disorder
_____	_____
_____	_____

SEXUALITY CONCERNS

BEHAVIORAL DEFINITIONS

1. History of sexual victimization due to the vulnerability that is caused by severe and persistent mental illness symptoms.
2. Bizarre sexual thoughts due to hallucinations, delusions, or other severe and persistent mental illness symptoms.
3. Engaging in high-risk behavior for sexually transmitted diseases (STDs) due to a lack of understanding about healthy sexual behavior.
4. Impulsive sexual acting out, or hypersexuality.
5. Sexual dysfunction due to the side effects of long-term psychotropic medication use.
6. Medical problems that are related to STDs.
7. Inadequate prenatal care due to homelessness, confusion, or other effects of mental illness symptoms.
8. Conflicts in sexual or romantic relationships due to bizarre behavior or other symptoms.

—. _____
_____
_____
—. _____
_____
_____
—. _____
_____

LONG-TERM GOALS

1. Increase resistance to sexual victimization.
2. Understand the effects of sexual behavior and increase the use of safer-sex practices.

3. Obtain the appropriate medical care that is related to the sexual behavior (e.g., prenatal care, birth control, and STD treatment).
4. Decrease the severe and persistent mental illness symptoms that precipitate sexual acting out.
5. Return to a normal libido and sexual functioning that is relative to the medication usage.
6. Normalized sexual or romantic relationship that is less affected by the symptoms of mental illness.

—. _____
   _____
—. _____
   _____
—. _____
   _____

SHORT-TERM OBJECTIVES

1. Identify the possible areas of sexuality concerns. (1, 2)
2. Verbalize the degree of comfort regarding discussing sexuality issues. (3, 4)
3. Describe the details of sexuality concerns. (5, 6, 7, 8)
4. Disclose the history of sexual abuse. (5, 6, 9, 10, 11)
5. Demonstrate a reduced emotional response to prior sexual abuse. (11, 12, 13, 14, 15)
6. Take steps to protect self from a continuation of current sexual victimization (10, 16, 17, 18, 19, 20)
7. Terminate sexually abusive or otherwise inappropriate behaviors toward others. (18, 21, 22, 58)

THERAPEUTIC INTERVENTIONS

1. Explore the client's history of sexual abuse, sexual dysfunction, deviant sexual practices, or vulnerability to sexual victimization.
2. Carefully review the client's medical records for information indicating sexuality concerns.
3. Present to the client inquiries into sexuality issues in a tentative, open manner, due to the highly personal and emotional nature of such issues.
4. Focus the client on voluntarily working on these issues, and that he/she is in control of how quickly or intensely these issues are addressed.
5. Request that the client identify the details of his/her

8. Verbalize an increased knowledge about human sexuality. (23, 24)

9. Take psychotropic medications consistently to decrease severe and persistent mental illness symptoms. (25, 26, 27)

10. Report on the side effects and the effectiveness of the psychotropic medications. (26, 27, 28, 29)

11. Present an improved self-image as a result of improved activities of daily living (ADLs) or personal appearance. (30, 31)

12. Report an improvement in social and romantic relationships. (32, 33)

13. Partner reports a decrease in tension within the relationship and within the family unit. (6, 34, 35, 36, 37)

14. Identify sexual dysfunction concerns. (6, 38, 39)

15. Resolve medical issues that inhibit sexual functioning. (29, 40, 41, 42, 43)

16. Decrease the likelihood of contracting STDs. (44, 45, 46)

17. Cooperate with an assessment for STDs. (47, 48)

18. Pursue a treatment for STDs. (49, 50)

19. List the pros and cons of parenthood. (51, 52)

20. Use contraception consistently. (46, 53, 54)

history of sexual difficulties, dysfunction, or confusion.

6. With the proper consent to release information, obtain additional information about sexuality concerns from the client's spouse, partner, or other family members.

7. Request that the client prepare a timeline reviewing his/her history of sexual involvement.

8. Focus the client on differentiating between the reality of the experience and the possible altered perception of reality due to severe and persistent mental illness symptoms; assess the client's reality testing.

9. Ask the client to describe his/her history of sexual abuse.

10. Educate the client about the definition of sexual abuse.

11. Provide the client with ample time to gradually express the story of the sexual abuse.

12. Review the common emotional, self-esteem, and relationship effects of sexual abuse with the client.

13. Assign readings from *The Courage to Heal: A Guide for Women Survivors of Child Sexual Abuse* by Bass and Davis or *Reach for the Rainbow: Advanced Healing for Survivors of Sexual Abuse* by Finney to assist

21. Verbalize a plan of reaction to possible pregnancy. (15, 55, 56, 57)

22. Verbalize an acceptance of self regardless of sexual identity. (15, 58, 59, 60, 61)

—. _____
   _____

—. _____
   _____

—. _____
   _____

the client in processing his/her feelings that are related to sexual abuse.

14. Assign and process written assignments from *The Courage to Heal Workbook: For Men and Women Survivors of Child Sexual Abuse* by Davis to help the client understand and resolve the emotional effects of sexual abuse.

15. Refer the client for ongoing psychotherapy with a therapist who is knowledgeable about sexual conflicts and chronic mental illness symptoms.

16. Ask the client about specific current situations in which he/she may be experiencing sexual assault or abuse.

17. Advocate for the client to obtain the needed supports that will remove him/her from an abusive situation (e.g., domestic violence shelter, protection order).

18. Report sexual victimization to the police or to an adult protective services agency, in accordance with agency guidelines and local legal requirements.

19. Assist the client in stabilizing financial and residential needs to decrease the likelihood of having to be dependent on a sexually or physically abusive partner. (See the Homelessness and the Financial Needs chapters in this Planner.)

20. Educate the client about self-defense strategies, such as those described in *Self Defense: Steps to Success* by Nelson.

21. Provide feedback to the client on his/her sexually inappropriate, and possibly illegal, behavior.

22. Refer the client to a sexual offender treatment group.

23. Educate the client about human sexuality through videotapes, books, and other literature (e.g., *All About Sex: A Family Resource on Sex and Sexuality* by Moglia and Knowles or *Sexual Health: Questions You Have . . . Answers You Need* by Reitano and Ebel).

24. Refer the client to a sex education group (e.g., see *Positive Partnerships: A Sexuality Education Curriculum for Persons with Serious Mental Illness* by Caldwell and Reynolds.

25. Refer the client to a physician or a psychiatrist for an evaluation of the need for psychotropic medication.

26. Educate the client about the use, expected benefits, and possible side effects of psychotropic medications.

27. Monitor the client's medication compliance and effectiveness.

28. Review the side effects of the medications with the client and the medical staff.

29. Educate the client about the sexual side effects of the prescribed medications so that he/she can make an informed decision about whether to use them.

30. Advocate for the client, with a psychiatrist, for the use of medications that reduce the likelihood of extrapyramidal side effects (EPSs).

31. Assist the client in increasing ADLs. [See the Activities of Daily Living (ADL) and the Independent Activities of Daily Living (IADL) chapters in this Planner.]

32. Refer the client to a support group for mentally ill adults.

33. Teach the client social skills that can be applied to a range of intimate relationships. (See the Social Skills chapter in this Planner.)

34. Educate the client's spouse/partner about mental illness symptoms and their impact on intimacy.

35. Assist the client's spouse/partner in resolving family needs that are not related directly to the client's mental illness symptoms (e.g., day care needs for their children, transportation needs, medical help, etc.), but that are increasing the tension level within the marriage.

36. Engage the client's spouse or partner in an active role in the client's treatment

(e.g., attending treatment meetings, providing feedback to the clinicians, or managing medications) as allowed by the client.

37. Refer the client and his/her spouse or partner for marital therapy that is related to ongoing problem areas, or to "inoculate" the relationship from future troubles.

38. Review typical sexual needs that may have been neglected due to mental illness symptoms.

39. Ask the client specifically about sexual dysfunction symptoms.

40. Refer the client for a complete medical evaluation that is especially focused on possible biochemical causes for sexual dysfunction.

41. Coordinate the recommended follow-up to the medical evaluation, including prescribed lab tests, new medications, or specialty evaluations.

42. Review sexual dysfunction concerns with the prescribing physician. Advocate with the physician for a psychotropic medication regimen that minimizes the impact on sexual libido and sexual functioning.

43. Assess the client carefully for decompensation, interpreting the sexual dysfunction as a precursor or a signal for crisis.

44. Educate the client about STDs and how to avoid them (e.g., abstinence, use of condoms).

45. Suggest that the client read material on STDs (e.g., *Sexually Transmitted Diseases: A Physician Tells You What You Need to Know* by Marr).

46. Provide the client with free condoms or refer him/her to an agency that provides them; teach the client about proper and timely use.

47. Educate the client about the communicable nature of STDs and the danger to future partners.

48. Refer the client to a public health facility or to a physician to test for acquired immune deficiency syndrome (AIDS) and other STDs.

49. Coordinate the client's treatment for STDs as medically indicated.

50. Refer the client who tests positive for the human immunodeficiency virus (HIV-positive) to an appropriate support group.

51. Review the possible motivations that are related to parenthood, which are prominent with mentally ill individuals (e.g., a redefinition of the client's self-concept from a "mentally ill individual" to a "parent," or a greater desire to maintain his/her psychological health).

52. Focus the client on the stressors that are related to parenthood (e.g., financial burdens, increased responsibility) that may exacerbate mental illness symptoms.

53. Teach the client about the correct and effective use of condoms, birth control pills, and other contraceptives.

54. Refer the client for birth control measures that are less likely to fail due to human error (i.e., Depo-Provera shots).

55. Provide the client with information regarding options that are available for reacting to pregnancy (e.g., abortion, release for adoption, keeping the baby).

56. Educate the client about, and emphasize the critical need for, discontinuing alcohol or street drug use if it is possible that the client is pregnant.

57. Inform the client's prescribing physician immediately if the client suspects that she might be pregnant.

58. Assist the client in identifying atypical sexual behavior, which is related to psychosis, mania, or other severe and persistent mental illness symptoms, as opposed to his/her typical sexual behavior or sexual orientation.

59. Validate the client's experience of additional stigmati-

zation or discrimination that he/she may have experienced because of being mentally ill *and* gay/lesbian.

60. Acknowledge that family and societal issues that are related to sexual orientation as a stressor may, indeed, exacerbate the symptoms; affirm the client's worth, regardless of his/her sexual identity.

61. Refer the client to a support group for those who are struggling with sexual orientation issues and mental illness concerns.

—. _____
   _____
—. _____
   _____
—. _____
   _____

DIAGNOSTIC SUGGESTIONS

Axis I:	297.1	Delusional Disorder
	295.xx	Schizophrenia
	295.70	Schizoaffective Disorder
	296.xx	Bipolar I Disorder
	296.89	Bipolar II Disorder
	293.xx	Psychotic Disorder Due to . . . [General Medical Condition]
	292.xx	Substance-Induced Psychotic Disorder
	302.71	Hypoactive Sexual Desire Disorder
	302.79	Sexual Aversion Disorder
	302.72	Sexual Arousal Disorder
	302.7x	Orgasmic Disorders

302.70	Sexual Dysfunction NOS
302.9	Sexual Disorder NOS
V61.1	Sexual Abuse of Adult
995.81	Sexual Abuse of Adult—Victim
_____	_____
_____	_____

SOCIAL SKILLS

BEHAVIORAL DEFINITIONS

1. Repeated bizarre or other inappropriate social behaviors.
2. History of repeated broken or conflicted relationships due to personal deficiencies in problem solving, maintaining a trusting relationship, or choosing abusive/dysfunctional partners/friends.
3. A pattern of social shyness, anxiety, or timidity.
4. Rude, angry, oppositional, or demanding behaviors toward peers and others.
5. Inability to establish, nurture, and maintain meaningful interpersonal relationships due to a failure to listen, support, communicate needs, or negotiate differences of opinion.
6. Estrangement from others due to the negative effects of psychotic symptoms (i.e., hallucinations, delusions, manic phases) on social interactions.
7. Complaints of loneliness, lost relationships, and a lack of friends or a social network to provide support during crises.
8. Lack of assertiveness, difficulty resisting peer pressure, or a deficiency in expressing needs or saying "no."
9. Lack of experience with or lack of an understanding of the social aspects of recreational/leisure activities.

—. _____
   _____
—. _____
   _____
—. _____
   _____

LONG-TERM GOALS

1. Develop an awareness of and an acceptance of social skills deficits.
2. Understand how chronic mental illness symptoms impact social skills and relationships.
3. Accept the need for and the usefulness of increasing social skills abilities.
4. Learn basic social skills techniques such as communicating needs, making requests, reading body language, and establishing eye contact.
5. Learn advanced social skill techniques such as assertiveness, active listening, and negotiation.
6. Establish or reestablish mutually satisfying, important interpersonal relationships.
7. Family, friends, and caregivers develop realistic expectations about the client's social capabilities.

—. _____
  _____
  _____
—. _____
  _____
  _____
—. _____
  _____

SHORT-TERM OBJECTIVES

1. Describe current social contacts. (1, 2, 3)
2. Identify positive and negative experiences in social interactions. (4, 5)
3. Acknowledge the presence of social skills deficits as a symptom of mental illness. (6)
4. Take the antipsychotic medication consistently as prescribed. (7, 8)
5. Report the side effects and the effectiveness of the

THERAPEUTIC INTERVENTIONS

1. Request that the client prepare a list of all important relationships, including friends, family, and treatment providers.
2. Develop a family genogram to assist the client in identifying important relationships in the family.
3. Review the client's list of important relationships, looking for those expected relationships that are omitted, and inquire about these.

medications to an appropriate professional. (9, 10)

6. Verbalize an understanding of the positive effects of the medication on social interactions. (10, 11)

7. Identify relationships that have been lost due to social skills problems. (3, 5, 12)

8. Describe those social skills that are desired but missing from the current repertoire. (13)

9. Increase the frequency of assertive behaviors. (14, 15, 16)

10. Identify a secondary gain that is received by continuing poor social skills functioning. (17, 18)

11. Cooperate with the cognitive assessment. (19)

12. Identify basic body language signals and state their meaning. (20, 21)

13. Increase the frequency of speaking with appropriate eye contact in social situations. (22, 23, 24)

14. Implement the conversational skills of asking questions and listening, which are used in basic social interactions. (25, 26, 27, 28)

15. Verbalize an understanding of the impact of psychotic symptoms on social interactions. (29, 30, 31)

16. Report instances of verbally accepting and acknowledging praise from others. (31, 32)

4. Ask the client to list two successful social interactions.

5. Ask the client to describe two painful social experiences that indicate the need for improved social skills.

6. Educate the client about the expected or the common symptoms of his/her mental illness, which impact upon social relationships (i.e., manic behaviors or negative symptoms of schizophrenia).

7. Arrange for a psychiatric evaluation to assess the need for antipsychotic or other psychiatric medication, and arrange a prescription, if appropriate.

8. Encourage the client to take the medications consistently.

9. Educate the client about the use of and the expected benefits of psychiatric medications.

10. Monitor the client's use of the medications, their effectiveness and compliance.

11. Assist the client in recognizing the positive impact of consistent use of the psychiatric medications on social interactions.

12. Ask the client to identify two situations in which his/her mental illness symptoms have contributed to problems in relationships.

13. Request that the client describe how he/she would like the relationship to work and what skills would

17. Invite others to join in a group activity. (33)

18. List group activities that would be enjoyable to share with family/friends. (34)

19. Participate in community- or agency-sponsored social/recreational activities. (35)

20. Share instances of experiencing social discrimination based on mental illness. (36, 37)

21. Practice making self-affirming statements to self daily. (38)

22. Implement relaxation techniques to decrease social anxiety. (39)

23. Family members express their emotions related to the client's past social skills deficits and mental illness symptoms. (40, 41)

24. Family members increase positive support of the client to reduce stress and to decrease the exacerbation of the primary symptoms. (42, 43)

25. Identify important relationships that have been lost and that could possibly be reconciled. (44)

26. List those who deserve an apology for previous relationship problems. (45)

27. Apologize/make amends for previous behavior that has offended others. (46)

have to be learned to achieve that ideal.

14. Ask the client to identify situations in which he/she would like to behave more assertively.

15. Teach assertiveness skills by using such books as *The Assertiveness Workbook* by Pfeiffer or *Assert Yourself* by Lindenfield.

16. Refer the client to an assertiveness training workshop, which will educate and facilitate assertiveness skills via lectures, assignments, and role playing.

17. Educate the client about secondary gain (e.g., allowances that others make, intimidation, lowered expectations, etc.) that accrues due to a lack of social skills.

18. Educate the client about passive-aggressive traits (e.g., playing the martyr, eliciting negative responses, etc.) and others' negative responses to such behavior.

19. Assess the client's cognitive ability via psychological testing such as the Weschler Adult Intelligence Scale, 3rd Edition (WAIS-III) or the Wide Range Achievement Test, 3rd Edition (WRAT-III), and evaluate the implications for social skills learning.

20. Assist the client in identifying three different body language messages from

__. _____

_____

__. _____

_____

__. _____

_____

preselected photographs (use materials from magazines, family photos, etc.).

21. Use role playing, modeling, and behavior rehearsal to teach the client how to accurately interpret body language signals.

22. Confront the client's lack of eye contact.

23. Encourage and reinforce the client's use of eye contact when speaking with others.

24. Use role playing and behavior rehearsal to practice eye contact during social interaction.

25. Give the client homework of developing a list of five topics in which he/she is interested, as well as five topics in which others seem to be interested.

26. Use role playing to practice asking questions about areas of interest, modeling eye contact, noninterruptive listening, and assertiveness in the process.

27. Assign the client to practice using listening and speaking skills in three social situations and review his/her successes and difficulties.

28. Refer to a self-help or peer-led support group for individuals with chronic mental illness to provide a supportive environment to continue the practice of conversation skills.

29. Monitor and give feedback to the client about areas in which mental illness symptoms may affect his/her thought process.

30. Assist the client in developing support from others by identifying trusted individuals who can provide feedback about the mental illness symptoms' effects on thoughts (e.g., delusions) and behavior (e.g., impulsiveness).

31. Assign the client homework of gaining feedback from others in three social situations.

32. Assign the client to be aware of and graciously acknowledge (without discounting) praise and compliments from others.

33. Role-play approaching others to ask them to be involved in a group activity.

34. Assist the client in identifying mutually satisfying social activities for himself/herself and friends/family members.

35. Encourage and facilitate the client's involvement in community- or agency-sponsored social/recreational opportunities (i.e., bowling, exercise groups, church groups, etc.).

36. Reframe instances of discrimination toward the client in community involvement as a fault of the discriminating individual or

group, while acknowledging the hurt that the client may experience.

37. Help the client identify previous rejections and process the pain that is related to these rejections.

38. Use a positive self-affirmation technique (i.e., the client writes from 6 to 10 positive statements about himself on 3-by-5-inch cards and reviews them several times per day) to increase the client's focus on positive characteristics that may draw others toward him/her.

39. Teach progressive muscle relaxation and safe-place visualization techniques to assist the client in decreasing his/her anxiety in social situations.

40. Encourage the family members to identify and vent about the client's past behavior and symptoms.

41. Coordinate a family therapy session to allow the family to express concerns, emotions, and expectations directly to client.

42. With the proper release of information, answer family questions about the client's mental illness symptoms and abilities.

43. Refer the client's family members to a community-based support group for loved ones of chronically mentally ill individuals.

44. Review the client's list of important relationships, processing which lost relationships can be salvaged, developed, or resurrected.

45. Assist the client in identifying those who have been hurt in these previous relationships.

46. Coordinate a conjoint therapy session for making an apology/making amends.

__. _____
   _____

__. _____
   _____

__. _____
   _____

DIAGNOSTIC SUGGESTIONS

Axis I:	297.1	Delusional Disorder
	295.xx	Schizophrenia
	295.0	Schizophrenia, Disorganized Type
	295.70	Schizoaffective Disorder
	296.xx	Bipolar I Disorder
	296.89	Bipolar II Disorder
	V61.9	Relational Problem Related to a Mental Disorder
	V62.81	Relational Problem NOS
	_____	_____
	_____	_____

SUICIDAL IDEATION

BEHAVIORAL DEFINITIONS

1. Recurrent thoughts or preoccupations with death.
2. Auditory command hallucinations that direct the client to harm himself/herself.
3. Recurrent ongoing suicidal ideation without any specific plans.
4. Ongoing suicidal ideation with a specific plan.
5. Recent suicide attempt.
6. History of suicide attempts that have required hospitalization or other direct intervention.
7. Positive family history for suicide or affective disorder.
8. Extreme impulsivity due to mania, psychosis, or other severe and persistent mental illness symptoms.
9. A significant increase in depressive symptoms (e.g., a bleak, hopeless attitude toward life), coupled with a recent increase in severe stressors (e.g., loss of a loved one, relationship problems, loss of a job/home).

__. _____
   _____
__. _____
   _____
   _____
__. _____
   _____

LONG-TERM GOALS

1. Stabilize the current suicidal crisis.
2. Terminate suicidal ideation.
3. Reestablish reality orientation.

4. Improve coping skills for crisis stressors.
5. Decrease severe stressors.
6. Reestablish a sense of hope for self and for the future.
7. Decrease affective disorder or other severe and persistent mental illness symptoms, returning to highest previous level of functioning.

—. _____
   _____
   _____
—. _____
   _____
   _____
—. _____
   _____

SHORT-TERM OBJECTIVES

1. Verbalize the current level of suicidal intent. (1, 2, 3, 4, 5)
2. Cooperate with a hospital and/or residential care if the urge for suicide is not controllable. (6, 7, 8)
3. Cooperate with a crisis care plan that includes 24-hour self-supervision. (9, 10)
4. Family/caregivers decrease lethal means that are available to the client. (11, 12)
5. Verbalize a commitment to a suicide prevention contract. (9, 13, 14)
6. Verbalize hopeful statements regarding the future. (15, 19, 47)
7. Follow through on commitments of the suicide prevention contract. (13, 14, 16, 17)
8. Agree to structure time with specific tasks and goals for the immediate fu-

THERAPEUTIC INTERVENTIONS

1. Question the client directly and openly about the presence of suicidal ideation.
2. Perform a risk assessment of the suicidal ideation, including the nature of the client's suicidal statement, specific plans, access to the means of suicide, and the degree of hope for the future. Focus on his/her statements rather than (flattened) affect, which may be influenced by other symptoms of his/her mental illness.
3. Arrange for psychological testing, including a test specifically designed to assess suicide lethality (e.g., the *Suicide Probability Scale* or the *Beck Scale for Suicide Ideation*).
4. Request feedback from family members, friends, or caregivers about the client's

ture that confirm a desire to live. (18, 19)

9. Verbalize an understanding that suicide is not a constructive solution to current stressors. (20, 21, 22, 23)

10. Caretakers, friends, and family members provide support and supervision to the client. (9, 18, 24, 25, 26)

11. Participate in an evaluation by a physician as to the need for medication to treat depression or psychosis. (27, 28, 29)

12. Report the side effects and the effectiveness of the psychotropic medications to the appropriate professional. (28, 29, 30)

13. Identify the stressors that led to decompensation and suicidal ideation. (1, 31, 32)

14. Process the emotions that are related to the stressors that contribute to suicidal ideation. (33, 34, 35)

15. Verbalize a willingness to tolerate the pain of passing negative emotions. (33, 36, 37, 38)

16. Verbalize a distinction between psychotic hallucinations/delusions and reality. (35, 39, 40, 41)

17. Report an increase in healthy thinking patterns replacing suicidal ideation. (42, 43, 44, 45, 46)

18. Identify specific, positive reasons to go on living. (43, 44, 47, 48)

suicidal ideation and symptom intensity.

5. Obtain clinical supervision or feedback from clinical peers regarding a necessary reaction to the client's current status.

6. Obtain immediate emergency medical care for any suicide attempt.

7. Coordinate an admission to a psychiatric hospital unit or a crisis residential program, which has a 24-hour, trained staff.

8. Contact/petition the appropriate court or legal entity to involuntarily admit the client to a psychiatric unit until his/her suicidal crisis is alleviated.

9. Develop and implement a crisis care plan, including supervision from caretakers, friends, and family.

10. Obtain positive feedback from the client about his/her willingness to proceed with the crisis care plan.

11. Advise the family/caregivers to remove lethal means from the client's access (i.e., take away firearms, knives, poisons, or other chemicals).

12. Recommend that the family/caregivers limit the amount of available medication to a less-than-lethal or harmful dose. Dispense daily if necessary.

19. Attend and participate in support and advocacy groups with other seriously mentally ill people. (49, 50)

20. Acknowledge substance abuse as a precipitating factor in decompensation and suicidal ideation. (51)

21. Implement problem-solving skills to resolve stressful conflicts. (52, 53)

22. Demonstrate improved social skills that can be used to build relationships and to reduce isolation. (54)

23. Keep in contact with the caregivers and the therapists through crises. (2, 55)

24. Agree to the terms of a long-term relapse prevention plan. (56, 57, 58)

25. Decrease the use of suicidal statements and gestures for secondary gain. (59, 60, 61)

__. _____
   _____
__. _____
   _____
__. _____
   _____

13. Write out a suicide prevention contract, including the commitment to contact the clinician or a 24-hour, professionally staffed crisis hotline. Request that the client sign the contract, then sign as a witness.

14. Explain, verbally and in writing, where the client or the caregivers should call or go to if the suicidal ideation persists or increases.

15. Provide verbal reinforcement to the client for a more positive focus, hopeful statements, and so on.

16. Utilize a written contract form to stipulate the client's agreement to no self-harm, as well as for planning his/her recovery (e.g., a signed treatment plan).

17. Offer to be available through phone contact should suicidal ideation increase.

18. Direct the client in developing structure to his/her time, scheduling the next several hours or days.

19. Remind the client to focus on the portion of himself/herself that wants to go on living. Point out that the client's interaction with the clinician is evidence that a part of him/her wants to live.

20. Normalize thoughts of suicide in the context of current problem areas. Validate the connection

between suicidal thoughts and emotional pain.

21. Talk openly and honestly about suicidal concerns, focusing on suicide as being a permanent solution (with devastating side effects) to what is often a temporary problem or emotional state.

22. Discourage the client from simply disregarding or denying suicidal ideation, reminding him/her that this approach generally increases the suicidal thoughts.

23. Acknowledge the fact that the client is ultimately in control of his/her suicidal activity. Reinforce the idea of suicide as an inadequate solution to stressors that the client temporarily views as intolerable.

24. Provide the client's caretakers, friends, and family members with information about available treatment options. Give feedback to family members based on their concerns.

25. With the appropriate permission to release information (or without permission if the crisis meets the legal requirement for breaking confidentiality to preserve life), give the client's caretakers, friends, and family members information about his/her specific suicidal ideation/concerns.

26. Direct the family or the caretakers to structure the environment to reduce the level
of stimulation to the agitated or psychotic client and
to reassure him/her of their
caring.

27. Refer the client to a physician or a psychiatrist for an
evaluation of the need for
psychiatric medication.

28. Educate the client about the
use and the expected benefits of psychotropic medications.

29. Monitor the client's medication compliance and effectiveness.

30. Review the side effects of
the medications with the
client and the medical staff.

31. Request that the client identify life circumstances that
have contributed to suicidal
ideation (i.e., the loss of a job
or a relationship, problems
getting along with others, or
hallucinations/delusions).

32. Assist the client in identifying how life stressors contribute to the suicidal
ideation.

33. Inquire about feelings of
hopelessness, anger, frustration, or sadness, which
may be contributing to suicidal ideation. Encourage
the client to vent these and
other emotions.

34. Provide the client with feedback and support related to

his/her emotional concerns.
Teach the client alternative
ways of expressing negative
emotions (e.g., writing,
drawing, physical activity,
or talking to a caregiver).

35. Encourage the client to
identify the hallucinations
and delusions as a symptom
of his/her mental illness.
Remind the client that the
emotional reaction that
he/she experiences due to
the hallucinations/delusions
is not reality based.

36. Assist the client in labeling
the suicidal behavior as an
avoidance of emotional pain.

37. Focus the client on the passing nature of his/her emotions, and the probability of
not having the negative
emotions at some point in
the future.

38. Assist the client in exter-
nalizing suicidal ideation,
emphasizing the use of suicidal impulses as a "warning sign" that other issues
need to be addressed.

39. Provide directives to the
client in clear, straightfor-
ward terms. Avoid philo-
sophical discussions or
"why" questions.

40. Assist the client in identifying the hallucinations and
the delusions that prompt
suicidal gestures.

41. Explore coping skills and
other interventions (e.g., re-

ducing external stressors, implementing distraction techniques, seeking out reality checking with caregivers, etc.), which will assist in decreasing psychotic thinking. (See the Psychosis chapter in this Planner.)

42. Help the client identify healthy coping practices that support more optimistic, upbeat thinking patterns (e.g., expressing emotions, social involvement, hobbies, or exercise).

43. Request that the client identify positive situations in his/her life.

44. When the client is in a stable period, request that he/she write a letter to himself/herself regarding how positive and healthy his/her life can be. Read this with the client when he/she has decompensated to a suicidal state.

45. Gradually decrease restrictions as the client displays healthy thought patterns and decreases suicidal ideation.

46. Monitor the client more closely for suicidal activity if his/her mood suddenly shifts from depressed and withdrawn to serene and at ease with previously overwhelming problems (i.e., he/she has decided to pursue a suicide attempt rather than to fight the stressors).

47. Focus the client on the positive aspects of his/her life. Ask him/her to provide a list of reasons to go on living.

48. Request that the client take the *Reasons for Staying Alive When You Are Thinking of Killing Yourself: Reasons for Living Scale* by Linehan.

49. Refer the client to a support group for individuals with mental illness.

50. Encourage the client's involvement in local awareness and advocacy groups or functions.

51. Assess the client for substance abuse and refer him/her to a substance abuse treatment program if necessary. (See the Chemical Dependence chapter in this Planner.)

52. Teach the client problem-solving skills through modeling and didactic training (e.g., focus on the positive, utilize negotiation, evaluate the pros and cons of alternatives, practice assertiveness).

53. Praise the client's use of healthy problem-solving skills.

54. Using modeling, role playing, and behavioral rehearsal to teach the client personal social skills or refer him/her to a social skills training camp. (See the Social Skills chapter in this Planner.)

55. Monitor the client more closely at possible crisis intervals (e.g., change in clinician, periods of loss, etc.).

56. Formulate a written, long-term plan with the client and his/her family for dealing with stressors/symptoms contributing to suicidal ideation, as well as specific plans for monitoring and supporting him/her. Coordinate this plan with all necessary supports or clinicians.

57. Gradually taper contact with the client to a maintenance level, or as indicated by other therapeutic needs.

58. Make personalized crisis cards, including a brief description of relapse prevention techniques, encouragement, and crisis contact numbers. Provide these cards to the client.

59. Point out to the client the powerful responses that a suicidal gesture can cause in others.

60. Assist the client in listing healthy ways to get his/her need for attention and affirmation of caring met that are not as dangerous and trust eroding.

61. With the proper release, develop a specialized treatment plan that can be distributed to other agencies that might be involved with a suicide attempt (e.g., local emergency room).

Focus this plan on how to decrease a secondary gain for suicidal gestures.

—. _____
   _____
—. _____
   _____
—. _____
   _____

DIAGNOSTIC SUGGESTIONS

Axis I:	295.xx	Schizophrenia
	295.10	Schizophrenia, Disorganized Type
	295.20	Schizophrenia, Catatonic Type
	295.90	Schizophrenia, Undifferentiated Type
	295.30	Schizophrenia, Paranoid Type
	295.70	Schizoaffective Disorder
	296.xx	Bipolar I Disorder
	296.89	Bipolar II Disorder
	297.1	Delusional Disorder
	293.xx	Psychotic Disorder Due to . . . [General Medical Condition]
	293.0	Delirium Due to . . . [General Medical Condition]
	294.xx	Dementia due to . . . [General Medical Condition]
	292.xx	Substance-Induced Psychotic Disorder
	298.9	Psychotic Disorder NOS
	_____	_____
	_____	_____

Appendix A

BIBLIOTHERAPY SUGGESTIONS

Activities of Daily Living

American College of Sports Medicine (1998). *ACSM Fitness Book*. Champaign, IL: Human Kinetics.

Aslett, D. (1984). *The Cleaning Encyclopedia: Your A to Z Illustrated Guide to Cleaning Like the Pros*. New York: Dell.

Bittman, M. (1998). *How to Cook Everything*. New York: Macmillan.

The Editors of *Good Housekeeping* (1989). *The Good Housekeeping Illustrated Cookbook*. New York: Hearst Books.

The Editors of the University of California-Berkeley (1995). *The New Wellness Encyclopedia*. New York: Houghton-Mifflin Co.

Pinkham, M., and Burg, D. (1993). *Mary Ellen's Complete Home Reference Book*. New York, NY: Three Rivers Press.

Sharkey, B. (1991). *Fitness and Health*. Champaign, IL: Human Kinetics.

Taintor, J., and Taintor, M. (1999). *The Complete Guide to Better Dental Care*. New York: Checkmark Books.

Aging

Beresford, L. (1993). *The Hospice Handbook*. New York: Little, Brown and Company.

Carter, R., and Golant, S. (1998). *Helping Someone With Mental Illness: A Compassionate Guide for Family Friends and Caregivers*. New York: Time Books.

Cassel, C., Ed. (1999). *The Practical Guide to Aging: What Everyone Needs to Know*. New York: New York University Press.

Cleveland, J. (1998). *Simplifying Life as a Senior Citizen*. New York: St. Martin's Griffin.

Hay, J. (1996). *Alzheimer's and Dementia: Questions You Have . . . Answers You Need*. Allentown, PA: People's Medical Society.

Helm, A., Ed. (1995). *E-Z Legal Advisor.* Deerfield Beach, FL: E-Z Legal Books.

Lebow, G., Kane, B., and Lebow, I. (1999). *Coping With Your Difficult Older Parent: A Guide for Stressed-Out Children.* New York: Avon Books.

Mueser, K. (1994). *Coping With Schizophrenia: A Guide for Families.* Oakland, CA: New Harbinger Publications.

Quinn, B. (1998). *The Depression Sourcebook.* Lincolnwood, IL: Lowell House/ NTC Contemporary Publishers.

Torrey, E. (1995). *Surviving Schizophrenia: A Manual for Families, Consumers and Providers.* New York: HarperCollins.

Anger Management

Copeland, M. (1992). *The Depression Workbook.* Oakland, CA: New Harbinger Publications.

Davis, M., Eshelman, E., and McKay, M. (1995). *The Relaxation and Stress Reduction Workbook, Fourth Edition.* Oakland, CA: New Harbinger Publications.

Rosellini, G., and Worden, M. (1997). *Of Course You're Angry.* Center City, MN: Hazelden Foundation.

Rubin, T. (1969). *The Angry Book.* New York: Macmillan.

Smedes, L. (1991). *Forgive and Forget: Healing the Hurts We Don't Deserve.* San Francisco: Harper.

Weisinger, H. (1985). *Dr. Weisinger's Anger Workout Book.* New York: Quill.

Williams, R., and Williams, V. (1993). *Anger Kills: 17 Strategies for Controlling the Hostility That Can Harm Your Health.* New York: Harper.

Woolis, R. (1992). *When Someone You Love Has a Mental Illness: A Handbook For Family Friends and Caregivers.* East Rutherford, NJ: Putnam Publishing Group.

Anxiety

Beck, A., Emery, G., and Greenberg, R. (1985). *Anxiety Disorders and Phobias: A Cognitive Perspective.* New York: Basic Books

Bourne, E. (1990). *The Anxiety and Phobia Workbook.* Oakland, CA: New Harbinger Publications.

Davis, M., Eshelman, E., and McKay, M. (1995). *The Relaxation and Stress Reduction Workbook, Fourth Edition.* Oakland, CA: New Harbinger Publications.

Flannery, R. (1992). *Post-Traumatic Stress Disorder: The Victim's Guide to Healing and Recovery.* New York: Crossroads.

Chemical Dependence

Beattie, M. (1992). *Codependent No More.* Center City, MN: Hazelden Foundation.

Fanning, P., and O'Neill, J. (1996). *The Addiction Workbook.* Oakland, CA: New Harbinger Publications.

Friends in Recovery (1995). *The 12 Steps—A Way Out.* Curtis, WA: RPI Publications.

Grateful Members (1994). *The Twelve Steps for Everyone . . . Who Really Wants Them.* Center City, MN: Hazelden Foundation.

Mooney, A., Eisenberg, A., and Eisenberg, H. (1992). *The Recovery Book.* New York: Workman Publishing.

Rosellini, G., and Worden, M. (1997). *Of Course You're Angry.* Center City, MN: Hazelden Foundation.

Depression

Appleton, W. (1997). *Prozac and the New Antidepressants.* New York: Plume.

Brower, S., and Brower, G. (1991). *Asserting Yourself: A Practical Guide for Positive Change.* Reading, MA: Perseus Books.

Burns, D. (1993). *Ten Days to Self-Esteem.* New York: William Morrow.

Burns, D. (1999). *Feeling Good: The New Mood Therapy.* New York: Avon Books.

Copeland, M. (1992). *The Depression Workbook.* Oakland, CA: New Harbinger Publications.

Golant, M., and Golant, S. (1996). *What to Do When Someone You Love Is Depressed: A Practical and Helpful Guide.* New York: Henry Holt and Company.

Helmstetter, S. (1986). *What to Say When You Talk to Yourself.* New York: Fine Communications.

Marsh, D., and Dickens, R. (1997). *Troubled Journey: Coming to Terms with the Mental Illness of a Sibling or Parent.* New York: Tarcher/Putnam.

Employment Problems

Bolles, R. (1999). *What Color Is Your Parachute? 2000.* Berkeley, CA: Ten Speed Press.

Fein, R. (1999). *101 Quick Tips for a Dynamic Resume.* Manassas Park, VA: Impact Publishing.

Lindenfield, G. (1997). *Assert Yourself.* New York: Harper Prism.

Morgan, D. (1998). *10 Minute Guide to Job Interviews.* New York: Arco Books.

Pfeiffer, R. (1998). *The Real Solution Assertiveness Workbook.* New York: Growth Publishing.

VGM Careen Horizons Editors (1997). *Resumes for the First Time Job Hunter (with Sample Cover Letters).* Chicago: NTC Publishing Group.

Family Conflicts

Carter, R., and Golant, S. (1998). *Helping Someone With Mental Illness: A Compassionate Guide for Family Friends and Caregivers.* New York: Time Books.

Court, B., and Nelson, G. (1996). *Bipolar Puzzle Solution: A Mental Health Client's Perspective.* Bristol, PA: Accelerated Development.

Medina, J. (1998). *Depression: How It Happens—How It's Healed.* Oakland, CA: New Harbinger Publications.

Mueser, K. (1994). *Coping With Schizophrenia: A Guide For Families.* Oakland, CA: New Harbinger Publications.

Quinn, B. (1998). *The Depression Sourcebook.* Lincolnwood, IL: Lowell House/ NTC Contemporary Publishers.

Torrey, E. (1995). *Surviving Schizophrenia: A Manual for Families, Consumers and Providers.* New York: HarperCollins.

Tsuang, M., and Faraone, S. (1997). *Schizophrenia: The Facts.* New York: Oxford University Press.

Financial Needs

Bierman, T., and Masten, D. (1998). *The Fix Your Credit Workbook.* New York: St. Martin's Griffin.

Bosley, M., and Gurwitz, A. (1993). *How to Get Every Penny You're Entitled to From Social Security.* New York: The Putnam Publishing Group.

Gelb, E. (1995). *Personal Budget Planner: A Guide for Financial Success.* Woodmere, NY: Career Advancement Center.

Social Security Administration (1995). *Red Book on Work Incentives: A Summary Guide to Social Security and Supplemental Security Income Work Incentives for People With Disabilities.* Washington, D.C.: Social Security Administration.

Walling, M. (1998). *Managing Your SSDI Benefits and Income Handbook.* West Chester, PA: Service Enhancement Associates.

Grief and Loss

James, J., and Friedman, R. (1998). *The Grief Recovery Handbook: The Action Program for Moving Beyond Death, Divorce and Other Losses.* New York: HarperCollins.

Kubler-Ross, E. (1997). *On Death and Dying.* New York: Macmillan.

Kushner, H. (1981). *When Bad Things Happen To Good People.* New York: Shocken Books.

Lafond, V. (1995). *Grieving Mental Illness: A Guide for Patients and Their Caregivers.* Toronto: University of Toronto Press

Smedes, L. (1982). *How Can It Be All Right When Everything Is All Wrong?* San Francisco: Harper.

Smedes, L. (1991). *Forgive and Forget: Healing the Hurts We Don't Deserve.* San Francisco: Harper.

Homelessness

Aslett, D. (1984). *The Cleaning Encyclopedia: Your A to Z Illustrated Guide to Cleaning Like the Pros.* New York: Dell.

Barrett, P. (1998). *Too Busy To Clean? Over 500 Tips and Techniques to Make Housecleaning Easier.* Pownal, VT: Storey Books.

Pinkham, M., and Burg, D. (1993). *Mary Ellen's Complete Home Reference Book.* New York: Three Rivers Press.

Portman, J., and Stewart, M. (1999). *Renter's Rights.* Berkeley, CA: Nolo Press.

Intimate Relationship Conflicts

Carter, R., and Golant, S. (1998). *Helping Someone With Mental Illness: A Compassionate Guide for Family, Friends and Caregivers.* New York: Time Books.

Colgrove, M., Bloomfield, H., and McWilliams, P. (1991). *How to Survive the Loss of a Love.* Los Angeles: Prelude Press.

Comfort, A., and Marcus, E. (1991). *The New Joy of Sex.* New York: Crown Publisher.

Court, B., and Nelson, G. (1996). *Bipolar Puzzle Solution: A Mental Health Client's Perspective.* Bristol, PA: Accelerated Development.

Gorman, J. (1998). *The Essential Guide to Mental Health.* New York: St. Martin's Griffin.

Joslin, K. (1994). *Positive Parenting From A to Z.* New York: Fawcett Columbine.

Kaplan, H. (1987). *The Illustrated Manual of Sex Therapy, Second Edition.* Bristol, PA: Brunner/Mazel.

Medina, J. (1998). *Depression: How It Happens—How It's Healed.* Oakland, CA: New Harbinger Publications.

Mondimore, F. (1999). *Bipolar Disorder: A Guide for Patients and Families.* Baltimore, MD: The Johns Hopkins University Press.

Mueser, K. (1994). *Coping With Schizophrenia: A Guide For Families.* Oakland, CA: New Harbinger Publications.

Phelan, T. (1995). *1-2-3 Magic: Effective Discipline for Children 2–12, Second Edition.* Glen Ellyn, IL.: Child Management, Inc.

Quinn, B. (1998). *The Depression Sourcebook.* Lincolnwood, IL: Lowell House/NTC Contemporary Publishers.

Roberts, A., and Padgett-Yawn, B., Eds. (1998). *The Reader's Digest Guide to Love and Sex.* Pleasantville, NY: The Reader's Digest Association.

Sinclair Institute. *Better Sex Videos. Vol. 1: Better Sexual Techniques, Volume 3: Making Sex Fun, Volume 8: You Can Last Longer: Solutions for Ejaculatory Control.* Available from Sinclair Institute, P.O. Box 8865, Chapel Hill, NC 27515. (800) 955-0888, Ext. 8NET2, or http://www.bettersex.com.

Torrey, E. (1995). *Surviving Schizophrenia: A Manual for Families, Consumers and Providers.* New York: HarperCollins.

Tsuang, M., and Faraone, S. (1997). *Schizophrenia: The Facts.* New York: Oxford University Press.

Woolis, R. (1992). *When Someone You Love Has a Mental Illness: A Handbook For Family Friends and Caregivers.* East Rutherford, NJ: Putnam Publishing Group.

Legal Concerns

Bergman, P., and Berman-Barett, S. (1999). *The Criminal Law Handbook: Know Your Rights, Survive the System.* Berkeley, CA: Nolo Press.
Carnes, P. (1983). *Out of the Shadows: Understanding Sexual Addiction.* Minneapolis, MN: Compcare.
Helm, A., Ed. (1995). *E-Z Legal Advisor: A Clear, Reliable Guide to Your Rights and Remedies Under the Law.* Deerfield Beach, FL: E-Z Legal Books.
National Alliance for the Mentally Ill (1999). *A Guide to Mental Illness and the Criminal Justice System: A Systems Guide for Families and Consumers.* Arlington, VA: The Alliance.
Ventura, J. (1996). *The Will Kit.* Chicago: Dearborn Financial Publishing.

Mania/Hypomania

Court, R., and Nelson, G. (1996). *Bipolar Puzzle Solution: A Mental Health Client's Perspective.* Bristol, PA: Accelerated Development.
Davis, M., Eshelman, E., and McKay, M. (1995). *The Relaxation and Stress Reduction Workbook, Fourth Edition.* Oakland, CA: New Harbinger Publications.
Gorman, J. (1998). *The Essential Guide to Mental Health.* New York: St. Martin's Griffin.
Hauri, P., and Linde, S. (1990). *No More Sleepless Nights: A Proven Guide to Conquering Insomnia.* New York: John Wiley & Sons.
Mondimore, F. (1999). *Bipolar Disorder: A Guide for Patients and Families.* Baltimore, MD: The Johns Hopkins University Press.
Torrey, E. (1995). *Surviving Schizophrenia: A Family Manual.* New York: Harper and Row.
Zammit, G., and Zanca, J. (1998). *Good Nights: How to Stop Sleep Deprivation, Overcome Insomnia and Get the Sleep You Need.* Kansas City, MO: Andrews McMeel Publishing.

Medication Management

Gorman, J. (1997). *The Essential Guide to Psychiatric Drugs.* New York: St. Martin's Griffin.
Preston, J., O'Neal, J., and Talanga, M. (1998). *Consumer's Guide to Psychiatric Drugs.* Oakland, CA: New Harbinger Publications.

Paranoia

Burns, D. (1993). *The Feeling Good Handbook.* New York: Plume.
Cudney, M., and Hard, R. (1991). *Self Defeating Behaviors.* San Francisco: HarperCollins.

Davis, M., Eshelman, E., and McKay, M. (1995). *The Relaxation and Stress Reduction Workbook, Fourth Edition*. Oakland, CA: New Harbinger Publications.

Ross, J. (1994). *Triumph Over Fear*. New York: Bantam Books.

Parenting

Carter, R., and Golant, S. (1998). *Helping Someone With Mental Illness: A Compassionate Guide for Family, Friends and Caregivers*. New York: Time Books.

Cline, F., and Fay, J. (1992). *Parenting Teens with Love and Logic: Preparing Adolescents for Responsible Adulthood*. Colorado Springs, CO: Pinion Press.

Court, B., and Nelson, G. (1996). *Bipolar Puzzle Solution: A Mental Health Client's Perspective*. Bristol, PA: Accelerated Development.

Davis, M., Eshelman, E., and McKay, M. (1995). *The Relaxation and Stress Reduction Workbook, Fourth Edition*. Oakland, CA: New Harbinger Publications.

Dobson, J. (1992). *The New Dare to Discipline*. Wheaton, IL: Tyndale House Publishers.

Gorman, J. (1998). *The Essential Guide to Mental Health*. New York: St. Martin's Griffin.

Joslin, K. (1994). *Positive Parenting From A to Z*. New York: Fawcett Columbine.

Larson, D., Ed. (1990). *Mayo Clinic Family Health Book*. New York: William Morrow and Company.

Miller, S. (1995). *When Parents Have Problems: A Book for Teens and Older Children with an Abusive, Alcoholic or Mentally Ill Parent*. Springfield. IL: Charles C. Thomas.

McKay, M., Fanning, P., Paleg, K., and Landis, D. (1996). *When Your Anger Hurts Your Kids: A Parent's Guide*. Oakland, CA: New Harbinger Publications.

Mondimore, F. (1999). *Bipolar Disorder: A Guide for Patients and Families*. Baltimore, MD: The Johns Hopkins University Press.

Mueser, K. (1994). *Coping With Schizophrenia: A Guide For Families*. Oakland, CA: New Harbinger Publications.

Phelan, T. (1995). *1-2-3 Magic: Effective Discipline for Children 2–12, Second Edition*. Glen Ellyn, IL.: Child Management.

Quinn, B. (1998). *The Depression Sourcebook*. Lincolnwood, IL: Lowell House/ NTC Contemporary Publishers.

Torrey, E. (1995). *Surviving Schizophrenia: A Manual for Families, Consumers and Providers*. New York: HarperCollins.

Tsuang, M., and Faraone, S. (1997). *Schizophrenia: The Facts*. New York: Oxford University Press.

Psychosis

Carter, R., and Golant, S. (1998). *Helping Someone With Mental Illness: A Compassionate Guide for Family, Friends and Caregivers*. New York: Time Books.

Court, B., and Nelson, G. (1996). *Bipolar Puzzle Solution: A Mental Health Client's Perspective.* Bristol, PA: Accelerated Development.

Mueser, K. (1994). *Coping With Schizophrenia: A Guide For Families.* Oakland, CA: New Harbinger Publications.

Torrey, E. (1995). *Surviving Schizophrenia: A Manual for Families, Consumers and Providers.* New York: HarperCollins.

Recreational Deficits

American College of Sports Medicine (1998). *The ACSM Fitness Book.* Champaign, IL: Human Kinetics.

Davis, M., Eshelman, E., and McKay, M. (1995). *The Relaxation and Stress Reduction Workbook, Fourth Edition.* Oakland, CA: New Harbinger Publications.

Helmstetter, S. (1986). *What to Say When You Talk to Yourself.* New York: Fine Communications.

Mondimore, F. (1999). *Bipolar Disorder: A Guide for Patients and Families.* Baltimore, MD: The Johns Hopkins University Press.

Sharkey, B. (1997). *Fitness and Health, Fourth Edition.* Champaign, IL: Human Kinetics.

Tsuang, M., and Faraone, S. (1997). *Schizophrenia: The Facts.* New York: Oxford University Press.

Self-Determination Deficits

Foxx, R., and Bittle, R. (1989). *Thinking It Through: Teaching a Problem-Solving Strategy for Community Living.* Champaign, IL: Research Press.

Gardner, N. (1996). *The Self-Advocacy Workbook.* Lawrence, KS: Kansas University.

Michigan Protection and Advocacy Service, Inc. (1998). *The Self-Advocacy Manual for Consumers.* Lansing MI: MPAS. www.mpas.org.

Pearpoint, J. (1993). *PATH: A Workbook for Planning Positive Possible Futures.* Toronto, Ontario: Inclusion Press.

Sexuality Concerns

Bass, E., and Davis, L. (1988). *The Courage to Heal: A Guide for Women Survivors of Child Sexual Abuse.* San Francisco: HarperCollins.

Caldwell, P., and Reynolds, S. (1994). *Positive Partnerships: A Sexuality Education Curriculum for Persons with Serious Mental Illness.* Tucson, AZ: Arizona Center for Training Services.

Davis, L. (1990). *The Courage to Heal Workbook: For Men and Women Survivors of Child Sexual Abuse.* San Francisco: HarperCollins.

Esser, A., and Lacey, S. (1989). *Mental Illness: A Homecare Guide*. New York: John Wiley & Sons.

Finney, L. (1992). *Reach for the Rainbow: Advanced Healing for Survivors of Sexual Abuse*. New York: Perigee Books.

Helmer, D. (1999). *Let's Talk About When Your Mom or Dad Is Unhappy*. Center City, MN: Hazelden.

Marr, L. (1998). *Sexually Transmitted Diseases: A Physician Tells You What You Need to Know*. Baltimore, MD: Johns Hopkins University Press.

Moglia, R., and Knowles, J. (Planned Parenthood) (1997). *All About Sex: A Family Resource on Sex and Sexuality*. Westminster, MD: Random House.

Nelson, J. (1991). *Self Defense: Steps to Success*. Champaign, IL: Leisure Press.

Reitano, M., and Ebel, C. (1999). *Sexual Health: Questions You Have . . . Answers You Need*. Allentown, PA: People's Medical Society.

Strong, S. (1996). *Strong On Defense*. New York: Pocket Books.

Social Skills Deficits

Pfeiffer, R. (1998). *The Real Solution Assertiveness Workbook*. New York: Growth Publishing.

Lindenfield, G. (1997). *Assert Yourself.* New York: Harper Prism.

Suicidal Ideation

Linehan, M., and Goodstein, J. (1983). "Reasons for Staying Alive When You Are Thinking of Killing Yourself: The Reasons for Living Scale." *The Journal of Consulting and Clinical Psychology* 51: 276–286.

Assessment Instruments

Abnormal Involuntary Movement Scale
Guy, W. (ed.) (1976). *ECDEU Assessment Manual for Psychopharmacology: Publication ADM 76-338*. Washington, D.C.: U.S. Department of Health, Education and Welfare.

Beck Scale for Suicide Ideation
Beck, A., and Steer, R. (1991). *Beck Scale for Suicide Ideation*. New York: The Psychological Corporation.

Marital Satisfaction Inventory
Snyder, D. K. (1979). *Marital Satisfaction Inventory (MSI): Administration Booklet*. Los Angeles: Western Psychological Services.

Marital Status Inventory
Weiss, R. L., and Cerreto, M. C. (1980). "The marital status inventory: Development of a measure of dissolution potential." *American Journal of Family Therapy*, 8, 80–86. Available from Dr. Robert L. Weiss, Department of Psychology, University of Oregon, Eugene, OR 97403, or rlweiss@oregon.uoregon.edu.

Suicide Probability Scale
Cull, J., and Gill, W. (1982). *Suicide Probability Scale.* Los Angeles: Western Psychological Services.
Weschler Adult Intelligence Scale—III
Weschler, D. (1997). *Weschler Adult Intelligence Scale, 3rd Edition.* New York: The Psychological Corporation.
Wide Range Achievement Test—3
Wilkinson, G. S. *The Wide Range Achievement Test—3.* Wilmington, DE: Wide Range, Inc.

Appendix B

INDEX OF DSM-IV CODES ASSOCIATED WITH PRESENTING PROBLEMS

Sedative, Hypnotic,
or Anxiolytic Abuse   305.40
  Medication Management

Sedative, Hypnotic,
or Anxiolytic Dependence   304.10
  Medication Management

Sexual Abuse of Adult   V61.1
  Sexuality Concerns

Sexual Abuse of Adult—
Victim   995.81
  Sexuality Concerns

Sexual Arousal Disorder   302.72
  Sexuality Concerns

Sexual Aversion Disorder   302.79
  Sexuality Concerns

Sexual Disorder NOS   302.9
  Sexuality Concerns

Sexual Dysfunction NOS   302.70
  Sexuality Concerns

Sibling Relational Problem   V61.8
  Family Conflicts

Social Phobia   300.23
  Anxiety
  Recreational Deficits

Specific Phobia   300.29
  Anxiety

Substance-Induced
Psychotic Disorder   292.xx
  Sexuality Concerns
  Suicidal Ideation

ABOUT THE DISK*

TheraScribe® 3.0 and 3.5 Library Module Installation

The enclosed disk contains files to upgrade your TheraScribe® 3.0 or 3.5 program to include the behavioral definitions, goals, objectives, and interventions from *The Severe and Persistent Mental Illness Treatment Planner.*

Note: You must have TheraScribe® 3.0 or 3.5 for Windows installed on your computer in order to use *The Severe and Persistent Mental Illness Treatment Planner* library module.

To install the library module, please follow these steps:

1. Place the library module disk in your floppy drive.
2. Log in to TheraScribe® 3.0 or 3.5 as the Administrator using the name "Admin" and your administrator password.
3. On the Main Menu, press the "GoTo" button, and choose the Options menu item.
4. Press the "Import Library" button.
5. On the Import Library Module screen, choose your floppy disk drive a:\ from the list and press "Go." Note: It may take a few minutes to import the data from the floppy disk to your computer's hard disk.
6. When the installation is complete, the library module data will be available in your TheraScribe® 3.0 or 3.5 program.

Note: If you have a network version of TheraScribe® 3.0 or 3.5 installed, you should import the library module one time only. After importing the data, the library module data will be available to all network users.

User Assistance

If you need assistance using this TheraScribe® 3.0 or 3.5 add-on module, contact Wiley Technical Support at:

Phone: 212-850-6753
Fax: 212-850-6800 (Attention: Wiley Technical Support)
E-mail: techhelp@wiley.com

---

*Note: This section applies only to the book with disk edition, ISBN 0-471-35962-9.

For information on how to install disk, refer to the **About the Disk** section on page 273.

WILEY
Publishers Since 1807